Smack-Dab
Divorce

Loved our years working together... efficiency and inspiration at its best.

Robin

Smack-Dab
Divorce

How I Bounced Back from Being Blindsided by My Husband's Affair

(During Our Attempt to Adopt, No Less)

Rachel Spry

ISBN: 978-0-578-83120-6

Cover design by 360 Media Group
Cover photos sourced from dreamstime.com
Page layout by Win-Win Words LLC

Printed in the United States of America

To my family and friends,
and to all the dogs in my life.

Contents

Introduction

I DIDN'T WRITE THIS BOOK AS A PERSONAL MEMOIR. It's only a backdrop to my own marriage and how, starting when I was still in high school, part of me lived with the realization that my own divorce was pretty much inevitable. I would get married, have kids, and then get divorced. Step One, Step Two, Step Three. That's an unhealthy outlook on life, and I'm guessing it's one shared by more children emerging from a broken family than any of us would want to believe.

At age twenty-two and about to become a bride to a man twelve years my senior, I was naïve—not cluelessly naïve—but not on equal footing with my husband-to-be in terms of awareness and being able to stand toe to toe with him. He was the older guy, already once-divorced, a successful professional. I was fresh out of college and not long removed from Greek house parties, spring break, and finals. I was headed into a marriage in which I would be clueless about what was going on in our marriage as well as *outside* our marriage (him, not me).

Thanks to therapy-assisted hindsight, here are some things I wish I had known before getting married:

- Develop a guard/warrior mindset for yourself!
- Define the repercussions if your needs are not being met in marriage.
- When things go bad in a relationship, a person has to head back in and clean things up for herself/himself.
- I should have expected and demanded the truth from him.
- I should not have let him change the subject and interrupt me.
- I should not have been so tolerant toward whatever happens.

In part, through therapy, I learned that tough love makes you stronger. I learned that I took for granted that David (not his real name, by the way) was happy. Neither of us listened to each other very well. As was told to me by my therapist, I suggest you forget about what other people have done or said in similar or not-similar situations when it comes to marriage and divorce. You are not competing with anyone else. You have to figure out what is right for you. Remove the idea that you have to figure this all out right now.

Although there was nothing funny or in any way comical about what I went through while I was going through the divorce, etc., my narrative tone at times is lighthearted. Reading about divorce doesn't have to be drudgery or feed into any depression you might be experiencing. My hope is that you will find some enjoyment in *Smack-Dab Divorce* as well as answers, guidance, and lots of encouragement.

Note to Readers

I am neither a legal expert nor a healthcare professional: any advice I give in this book should not be construed as legal/medical advice. My intent is to show you—especially if you are contemplating divorce, going through divorce, or in post-divorce recovery—that you can do this, and you can be smart and prepared for it. I was neither. I believe the experience and insights gleaned from my marriage and divorce, and which I bring to you, can help you. Note, too, that many of the names of people (including mine) and some of the locales have been changed for the sake of privacy and protection of possibly sensitive information. Other than that, all information in this book is truthful and correct to the best of my knowledge.

— Author

Smack-Dab
Divorce

1

Busted!

I GUESS THIS IS WHERE I SHOULD SAY I DON'T KNOW WHAT GOT INTO ME THAT MORNING, BUT THAT WOULD BE UN-TRUE. I do know what got into me, and now I needed to get it out and into the open. Something pushed me out of bed that morning. It was time for me to confront my husband, David, and weasel an admission out of him, one that I dreaded hearing but one that I now suspected to be the whole truth and nothing but the truth. So help him, God.

It was early May, a surreal time for us. We had just moved into our new California home in a cozy, upscale community in northern California. David and I had arrived there about six months earlier, and now we were in the process of freshening up the house. That included painting the walls; later, our plan was to put down new, hand-scraped hardwood flooring. Only now, the proverbial ceiling was about to come crashing down, and my world was about to fall to pieces.

From eight in the morning until late afternoon, we had workers in the house. It was a mess, but at least the mess around the house was evidence of progress. Our new house was about to get a lot nicer, comfier, and cozier with our nifty spiffs, sprucing things up and giving us the promise of a home sweet home that would be all ours to enjoy at all hours, if we so chose.

I awoke that morning with the realization that I had to confront my husband. It was in my head waiting for me when I sat up in bed. I had to ask him a question, one that definitely would elicit a right answer or a wrong answer, nothing in between.

When I walked into the kitchen, David was about to head out the back door to go to work. He had the sliding glass door pulled open and was straddling it, one foot inside the door, the other out on the back patio which went around the pool. The timing was impeccable, as this was usually the time I would take the dogs out for their morning walk. Dogs operate on an internal clock calibrated better than those inside humans, but the dogs were going to have to wait another few minutes. David would occasionally walk the dogs himself, but not this morning.

I walked across the floor, right up to David, looked him in the eye, and asked him, "Are you having an affair?" There was no pause, no catch in my throat, no uncertainty about shoving that question into his face. At that point, I didn't *really* think that he was having an affair. I just wanted to have a conversation with him to see where it went.

"No!" he said immediately, although I saw something in his eyes. Something different. He still hadn't moved—just one foot in, one foot out, straddling the threshold. What I saw in his eyes was something different than a "no."

"Are you having an affair?"

Again, it was no. No, no, no. Denial, denial, denial.

"I have to get to work; I have a meeting at eleven," he said, trying to move through the door, me still standing in front of him. He was always moving, always having to get somewhere. Bigshot executive working for a bigshot business. In retrospect, the constant movement equaled not having to address real unresolved issues within him. Once he was through the door, he would have to walk across the patio and around the pool to get to the garage on the other side of the house, in back.

I just remember thinking, *He's done something, and I don't know what it is.*

"I'll come home after the meeting and then we can talk."

I knew full well he wouldn't be coming right back after the meeting.

He was still at the door. Then he started to talk, telling me that there was something he would talk to me about, but again said that he would be back after his meeting.

Oh, no, I thought, *throw me a morsel so he can get out the door, and that will hold me over until he gets back.*

Then . . . "It wasn't anything—just one night in the back of a car."

It turned out that wasn't true, either.

Scumbag, lying son of a bitch!

The Truth, Please

I look back on that morning confrontation, and I regret demanding the information from him. It put him on the spot. Don't construe that as sympathy for him; it's not. It's bad strategy in terms of what I really needed to get out of him, which was the truth. His being in a rush to get out the door only to be put on the spot shifted him into defensive mode, not the best place to be for me to get the truth out of him.

The information came out in drips and drabs, some of it true, some of it not true. At the time, I didn't know the difference. After a few minutes of this, he said, "I'm going to work," although he was still standing there. He was trying to end the conversation, or at least put it on hold until after he got back who knows when.

I went back inside, and the hot, pent-up anger was spilling out of my ears. I needed to do something. I was pissed but not out of control. Not totally in control, either, but in control enough to break something without hurting anyone or causing damage that I would regret as soon as I did it.

We had been collecting these Versace Rosenthal plates—nice stuff. They were definitely on the higher end of our china collection, not the sort of stuff we pulled out when grilling steaks or hamburgers. I grabbed one off the wall and slammed it on the floor, two-handed, and it went all over the place. It got his attention. He went and got the dustpan and small broom and quickly cleaned it up, and then it was off to work, finally. Out the door for real this time. And with that, our marriage had hit the rocks.

4

'You Must Leave Before I Freak Out!'

Surprisingly, I was able to remember a lot of what I did the rest of the day; it wasn't just a blur. The main thing was that while my head was in a different place, somewhere between the backseat of that car and the ozone, I can remember the painter arriving a few minutes later and me asking her to leave, "because I just found out that my husband is having an affair." No sense in keeping it a secret.

"But I really can't leave because I have this job to do and a certain amount of time to finish it before I have to get on to my next job."

"No, you must leave before I freak out!"

She was counting on that job, and it took her a while to gather her stuff and leave. As soon as she was gone, I immediately called my mom and my sister, Corinne. I also called my aunt Bonnie, who told me the first thing I needed to do was to get a lawyer and to get my own credit card. I heard all this and was taking it all in, but what I remember is just being out of my mind.

Corinne is almost five years younger than I; growing up she had always been the tag-along, little kid sister, but at this point in our lives—we were both in our thirties by now—things had pretty much balanced out between us. She had been married several years, and she had seen enough stuff with David to have her suspicions about him, enough for her to start in on the "I told you so" less than a minute into our phone conversation.

What follows is Corinne in her own words, recalling the day I confirmed an affair:

"In the months leading up to Rachel's confrontation with David at the back door, I had suspected this—that he was having an affair," Corinne says. "What I didn't know was that she was going to confront him about it. Something just came over her to do it, and once she called and told us about it, that he had admitted the thing about what went on in the backseat, I remember thinking, *This is just the tip of the iceberg*. Rachel was very much in shock, and yet she knew so little that first day.

"I had told her for a long time that I thought something was going on, but I remember her not believing it. She never said, 'I think you're right.'

"I never trusted him and never liked him—just a slime ball. His personality from the start was just kind of slimy. Not a man of high integrity. Maybe he was a bit in the beginning, but it quickly went downhill."

So, What's Next?

Corinne is right; I didn't ever believe there was an affair going on. Even when he told me about the backseat sex, I was discounting it because I didn't understand how big this actually was—it turns out, obviously, it was about more than just one round of a backseat romp.

During those phone calls with my mom and sister that day—I'm not even sure if those were separate calls or together with them both at the same time—they were asking, "What are you going to do next?" And I'm telling them, "I don't even know what I'm doing *now*." My brain was all over the place.

It's not like you have a battle plan—or at least a grocery list of tasks to be checked off in the event you get blitzed with the news that your husband is out screwing someone else—stuffed in your purse ready to yank out at moment's notice. Hindsight says I should have at least suspected something. Corinne sure did.

One thing I learned from this: If you suspect your partner is having any sort of an affair, fling, or whatever you want to call it, sit down and at least write out a list of things you would need to be prepared to do if and when you ever find out something is going on. Think it through logically while you have your head on straight, even if you hate the thought of doing it. Know what to do with the shit before it hits the fan. Like they say in the Boy Scouts, "Be prepared." I wasn't.

Through all this I learned what it meant to be processing breaking news about your husband's illicit sexual activity at the same time you are flipping out. The adrenaline starts pumping and your stomach is churning. Keep in mind, I hadn't even heard the half of it yet. It's like my head was a big rock-hard mass and thoughts were bouncing off it. Nothing was getting through and taking up residence.

I couldn't process what people were saying to me because I was traumatized. Absolutely devastated. The fact that David wouldn't stand still long enough while straddling that stupid door to really tell me what was going on made me even angrier. I'm like, *Duh, where have you been for the last six months, Rachel? How did you not know this was going on?*

Among the few rational thoughts that day that managed to penetrate the force field surrounding my brain was remembering how many times we had discussed David's father having had an affair years earlier. I probably found this out after we had been engaged.

When I think back now to who David is and what had shaped him, that was a turning point for him. I was trying like hell to understand how he could have done all the things he did in terms of having the affair and keeping it from me. Meanwhile, he must have been telling his more-significant other that he loved her all those times that he had been seeing and "sleeping" with her. What his dad had done and how he did it definitely had had an effect on David, giving him the green light to just go for it without any apparent hesitation or remorse. Like father, like son.

The rest of that day was a lot of phone calls and me waiting around for him to come back home, which he never did, according to his pledge to come home after his 11:00 A.M. meeting. That should have put him home at around 1:00 P.M. He ended up getting home around seven or eight.

While waiting, I walked the dogs, again, saw one of my brand-new neighbors outside, and told her what was going on. She immediately gave me the name of her son's therapist.

I'm like, *Hell, I don't know anything or anyone, so I'm going to call her son's therapist, because why not?* And that's what I did. When I got the therapist on the phone, she told me she wasn't taking on any new clients. I needed to talk to her; that was the only thought registering at that point. "I just can't even describe how I feel," I said. She asked me to talk a little more about that. So I rambled on a little more about what David had done and who we were and how we had just moved there.

She saw me that afternoon for an hour-long session.

In her office, it was all venting by me, pouring out my guts, trying to get to the bottom of it all, wanting David to answer more questions and explain the who, what, why, and how about what was going on between him and this other woman. I wanted to know everything. I needed to know everything. My curiosity was insatiable.

"You don't need all that information," the therapist told me.

"Yes, I do need that information."

I knew it was going to be hurtful to hear all that, but I was determined. I couldn't help feeling that way. It was not my choice. I was out of control in my mind in need of that information.

"Why are you going to compound the hurt you now feel with detail?"

I was consumed by it—the curiosity. And this was one cat that wasn't going to be killed by it.

"Your home has to be your oasis," my therapist told me. "It has to be your peaceful place."

One good thing was that her office wasn't far from our house—just ten or fifteen minutes. For me, it was just angry driving. Just numb, really, both going and returning.

Martini Time

I was ready to hear the rest of it when David got home that day; I needed to hear it from beginning to end. All I had from that morning were those drips and drabs.

Before he got home, though, at one point I tried to call the girlfriend, Avery . . . Avery Martini. David had mentioned her name during those ten to fifteen minutes in the morning. She had a job back East at the company where David used to work, and, apparently, I had met her before. When David mentioned her name, he said it in such a way as to assume I knew whom he was talking about. He was still throwing out pebbles for me to chase after. I called the company—not exactly sure what I would say once I got her on the phone, but you can be sure it wasn't going to be good.

It turns out she wasn't there, at least not that day. Either she was out or at lunch . . . something. The only thing I knew for sure was that she wasn't screwing my husband—at that moment. I did end up talking to her sometime later, but that's for another day and perhaps for another chapter, if I still feel like talking about her when I get there.

I didn't know this girl. Somewhere in all this, I called a doctor to make an appointment to be tested for AIDS and any other STDs.

When David got home that night, he came in through the back door. I was in the kitchen. By now, I was starting to feel the gravity of how serious the affair was. That—combined with not knowing all the tawdry details and his indifference toward me—was just cutting

10

right through me. I still remember using the word *fuck* to describe what he and Avery had done, and he didn't like that reference at all. That told me he thought he was in love with her, and that just took my pain level up one more notch.

In my head, the images of them together were tormenting me. Within a week I went to the doctor to get a prescription for Ambien so that I could sleep better at night.

When David got home, finally, it was clear that he had been drinking, and it was, "I can't do any of this right now. I have to get some sleep, and then I have to get up early. I have a lot going on tomorrow."

Join the club, pal.

And, oh yeah, our efforts to adopt a child were now on hold. Permanent hold.

2

Love & Marriage

WHEN A YOUNG LADY GOES OUT ON THE TOWN WITH HER FRIENDS, it's usually with the idea she might meet a smart guy with a decent sense of humor. If he's cute, all the better. It also helps if he is single, and there's no harm in him having money and the willingness to spend it on a girl.

It's a known fact that most guys out on the town are on the prowl. If they are not expecting a one-night stand, they at least expect to end that night's hunting expedition with a phone number and perhaps a kiss on which to build something bigger and better.

Women are similar in some respects. Yes, we are doing some hunting of our own—I wouldn't go so far as to call it "prowling"—but we have a somewhat different set of expectations. It *might* include throwing an interesting guy a bone (a kiss) and a phone number, but that is no sure thing. I sure as heck know that I was no sure thing, but I always did have my eyes and, more importantly, my ears open if prospects warranted it. But I wasn't looking to meet anyone.

By now I was out of college, back home in New Jersey full-time, and working for that court-reporting firm that a college friend had helped line up for me. One night one of my friends called me up and said, "Let's go out tonight and party . . . drinks are only a dollar." I was all in, telling my friend, "I'm there." You mean I can drink all the Planter's punches I want for a dollar apiece? That's awesome.

My friends and I met up at a bar in Morristown (New Jersey), and we sat at the bar, with music playing. Within minutes I had my first Planter's punch, and life was good. It wasn't long before this guy walked up to me, pointed at me, and said. "I'm going to dance with you before the night is over." My first thought was, *Why in the hell aren't you asking me to dance right now? Why put it off?* We were already well into conversation, and he was charming and witty. So far, so good. I'm thinking, *This is one guy I might not mind chasing me until he catches me.*

I could tell that he was a hard worker, probably quite successful at whatever he did. He was always making reference to where he was traveling for his work, what he was doing, and—again—how hard he worked. He sounded sincere, and I was interested. *Not* infatuated, just interested, certainly worth a second look and a long conversation.

Rachel, Meet David

I was only twenty-two—I had him pegged for about ten years older than me. I also noticed that we were about the same height, around five feet, six inches. As young as I was, I was not well-versed in the ways of the world, as the saying goes, at least not in the way I should have been.

When I met David, I really wasn't dating anyone. I had just moved back from Florida and was reconnecting with high school and college friends. I was working at the court-reporting firm about an hour and a half away. In doing all this, I was going back and forth on the Garden State Parkway, hitting two or three toll booths going and coming.

One time I remember going through one of the toll booths on the way to work and seeing a sign that said, "Tokens for Sale." Well, I'm thinking, *I've **got** to get some tokens before the price goes back up.* I get to work and I'm telling people about the sale on tokens. I later told David, and he just started laughing. He pointed out to me that the sign meant that tokens were *for* sale, not *on* sale at a discount.

There I was, believing I was going to get a deal on tokens, and I was shocked when I learned what the sign really meant. I felt stupid and naïve, but what struck me more than that was how hard David just laughed at me. I didn't think about his manner so much at the time, but years later, as our marriage began to unravel, I remembered that moment as one among many, many signs of the lack of respect he had for me, for everyone, really.

The long and short of it is that I finally did dance with David that night. The bar was quite popular. They not only had the music, they also had a deejay, and that was fun. What shocked me the first time I danced with David wasn't just how short he was but also how this guy had so much confidence for a guy his size. He definitely had the Napoleon complex. Something to prove. "Don't mess with me." Yeah, that's the vibe I got from him.

A couple of days went by after our first meeting, and off he was, traveling to Washington, D.C. Then he called me and asked me out for the following weekend. It turns out he was already an assistant general counsel for a fairly large company—having gotten his J.D. in his mid-twenties. He was always traveling and talking about his travels and where he would be going next. I really enjoyed being with him and loved listening to all his stories.

About ten years later, here is a brief segment of what I wrote about David in my journal, recalling my early impressions of him and fast forwarding to where we were around the time that I confronted him about an affair and got him to admit to it. Bits and pieces of my journal entries throughout this book have been slightly altered here in keeping with the privacy parameters I noted in the introduction:

> I met David just a few months after I graduated from college. He was entertaining, hardworking, and smart. We had such fun dating, meeting each other's friends and families, and me trying sushi for the first time. I felt immediately at ease when I was with him, probably due to the premature death of my father at age forty-seven, less than a year before. At age twenty-two, I had no idea who I was or what I needed from a relationship. (After we were married) I relied on him for ways to keep our marriage strong and establish our traditions. In other words, I allowed him to be in charge . . .

16

Our early married life consisted of healthy habits, such as working outside together on the weekends, fishing in the pond, going to bed together, waking up together, and entertaining our family and friends over the weekends and holidays. Being together felt good. At a young age, he was given a great deal of responsibility and quickly rose to the top of the heap.

Later:

Of course, there were red flags. Instead of the young, fun-loving guy I met ten years earlier, David was becoming highly critical of everyone around him. He was allowing himself to be steered off course and becoming distracted by technology and pretty, young girls. He was beginning to be, or had always been, lacking self-confidence and controlling.

Remembering back to when I was twenty-two, that time in my life right after I had graduated was so peaceful and calm. David gave me peace of mind in the early parts of our relationship. He seemed to know how to make the right decisions, as he was able to operate on a different level of problems, as well as solutions, than I had ever had to deal with. A lot of my focus had shifted to him, obviously—whom he would be meeting with next, where his next trip would take him, what his next steps in life would be, stuff like that. It was all about him, which became less and less charming as the months and years went by. He lived about an hour away from me, in Chatham, New Jersey. Naturally, I spent a lot of time there with him and his friends.

I had a good job working for the court-reporting firm. One of the bennies, for me at least, was that my daily commute to work took me closer to David's house. I didn't have to make that big, sometimes snowy trek back down the Garden State Parkway. Oftentimes, after work, I would just go straight to his house, we'd go out to dinner, and I'd spend the night. The next morning I'd start out at a little deli, where I would get a bowl of hot, delicious soup and just coast back in to work.

Soon the conversation between David and me turned to Memphis. He'd been offered a job there that entailed a nice promotion for him. I took a trip there with him, and then it was time for him to take the job and time to move. Here he was, in his mid-thirties, and everything was making perfect sense. He would be working just across the state line, in Mississippi. I remember going down there in February and thinking, *Omigosh, this is a different world*. But it was the kind of different that I liked; for one thing, there wasn't four inches of ice covering the ground.

Making the First Move

When we started looking for homes, it was amazing to see what we could buy—it was a stunning difference. The next step was that if I was going to move from New Jersey, and we were going to live together, we would have to get engaged. I think I was the one who initiated it, although it was not an ultimatum. I simply said, "It's a huge move, and I'm leaving my family and a good job behind. We are at that point where we could take that next step." He had been first to tell me he loved me, while dancing after dinner one evening.

I was totally comfortable with him. Everything was moving along just as I had always wanted. He was well-liked and very entertaining . . . at least on the outside. It always seemed like people wanted him around. I had seen him around some of his coworkers, as well as his friends outside of work, in a variety of social settings, and he was always the icebreaker, the guy who got the fun started. I was impressed, and his ease socializing with other people put me further at ease with him as well as the people he knew in his own orbits.

David was an amazing storyteller—something he had gotten from his mom, a lost art. Between the stories and the jokes, I had never met anyone like him. It was all so much fun. Ah, the pleasures of youth and being in love. I was enjoying the ride, in love with a guy—not yet feeling the punch in the gut that awaits marriage to a spouse who is sneaky, secretive, and engaging in the occasional back-seat romp.

Wait, I'm sorry, this was supposed to be a fun chapter full of gladness, joy, house hunting, and engagement rings—everything you picture when you think Love & Marriage. So no jumping ahead to the slow-motion train wreck. Let me get back on track with the pre-mess bliss.

With him already in Memphis and me back in New Jersey, I had started packing and going through all my worldly possessions, carefully putting them in boxes before sealing them in preparation for shipping. It hit me that I had started to acquire some nice little things. Whatever trepidation I felt leaving home to go halfway across the country to live with a guy I hadn't known a year earlier was more than offset by my love for him and the excitement of a new adventure.

The company I had been working for threw a going-away party for me, and I ended up with a lot of beautiful gifts. One was a big Waterford vase and some other smaller Waterford-type things, all of which I packed into boxes myself. By the time we got to Memphis, though, a lot of that stuff had shattered, which I guess was a harbinger of how things would eventually come crashing down in our marriage.

By this time, David had returned east to help me pack and get ready for the move. On one of those nights we went out for dinner. We were walking Madison, New Jersey, when we came across a little jewelry shop that had a lot of pieces on display in a window, previewing an upcoming estate sale.

We stopped and looked in the window—more like gazed, in my case—and we spotted an engagement ring. It was a gorgeous solitaire diamond that had belonged to someone else (it's an estate sale, after all). I should have known what was going on when he said he thought we could get a good deal on this. So we decided I would go to the jewelry auction. When it came time for the auction, I tried on the ring. I also had my paddle and a blank check from him. Fun!

The bidding on the ring seemed to last an hour—for just this one little ring. A lot of people were bidding on it, and the ring turned out to be the most hotly contested item for the entire auction. I wasn't going to let it go, however. There was a couple behind me that couldn't have been more than eighteen years old—although I was all of twenty-three, at that having just had a birthday. At first there were something like four or five bidders, and it came down to between me and the young couple behind me. Out of the corner of my eye I could see their paddle keep going up, and I'm thinking *There's no way this is happening.* Patty, a good friend since second grade, was there with me, egging me on.

The bidding had started at fifteen hundred dollars, and I ended up winning it at thirty-three hundred. The most amazing part to me was being able to write a check that big. A bonus to all this was the bottle of champagne that went to the winner, after which Patty and I went out to eat and to celebrate. I also called David immediately after the bidding was over to tell him I had won. Hearing this, he said, "I had no question that you were going to get the ring, but you really didn't win anything; we had to pay for this." That's David—always a reference to money at every turn—the first such turn of many that would come.

He came back up to New Jersey the next weekend. I showed him the ring, and he proposed. He was not a get-down-on-one-knee kind of guy, though. It was more a business transaction than a romantic event. It was like after our first date—he had shaken my hand like we had just finished a business meeting. Even when he introduced himself to someone, he would say his first name twice: "Hello, I'm David . . . David Franken." There was something pretentious about it. Even James Bond has the coolness to put his own twist to the repeated-name bit, starting out with his last name first. David wasn't cool. He was always businesslike, and a handshake was always involved. I prefer the Bond approach to making introductions.

It was time for me to leave New Jersey and meet up with him in Memphis. I had my ring, then came the good-bye party at work, and then it was a heartfelt farewell to my friends. I left my car there for my mother to use and then went to the airport with Mom and my sister.

I made the move in May or June and spent the summer in Memphis looking for a teaching job. What I had was an early-childhood degree from the University of Lynchburg—I just didn't have the student-teaching part yet.

David ended up buying a five-thousand-square-foot home on five acres with a pond. He did all this while we were in Florida on a business trip together; there he is on the phone, with me by the pool, saying, "OK, we'll buy the house." I had seen it when we had flown down in February to meet everyone he would be working with and to look at homes.

Once we got moved in, we did a lot of work around and to that house. It had been built by a former race car driver whose dad was known for building churches, which is why it had a big steeple with great rooms and beams, and it was beautiful. And here I was, twenty-three. And living in this big house. Wow.

We quickly fell into our respective routines—him working as the general counsel at a (new) big company just over the state line in Mississippi and me at a private school just a stone's throw from Graceland.

The routine wasn't just about getting up at the same time each weekday morning and going to our jobs five days a week. It also meant putting in the time to get things done around the house, and that was a lot of work—hard work. There was also the matter of making dinner every night—exclusively my job. He didn't help—of course not. His thing was working outside, on what we called the "Back Forty" on the other side of the pond, where he had a big barrel that he would use to burn twigs and branches. After a while, he had cleared out the whole place, and it looked great.

Four's a Crowd

About six months after I had moved to Tennessee to join David, my mother and sister moved there as well. The plan was for them to stay at the house until they found their own place in which to live.

They stayed mostly upstairs in the house. But I do remember a few jabs from David here and there, things like, "Why are they here, and when are they leaving? If we move again, are they going to follow us all over the place? I am not marrying your mother and sister; I'm marrying you." I think he felt threatened, and I believe none of this would have happened had my dad still been alive.

David and I had the master bedroom suite downstairs, and Mom's and Corrine's rooms were upstairs—they had plenty of space. All this time David and I were building our lives together, and I never thought for a minute that there was anything wrong with this arrangement, especially knowing it was only temporary.

23

I know I might be naïve in saying this. There's a lot I wish I had known back then about the ways of the world. I think my instincts were intact, they just weren't sharpened. Perhaps you rely mostly on your parents for that sort of thing, and now I had one fewer parent, newly deceased.

Anyway, Mom and Corinne moved out after two weeks because they couldn't take him anymore, either. This stuff works both ways. They just expedited the process of finding a place to live in the Memphis area, and they ended up finding a nice townhome. It was great.

In general, there were no other distractions in our lives, and everything was working out nicely. There was David's travel with me going along for the ride, and whatever else might be in store. Hawaii, Sea Island, Miami, you name it—where he went, I went. There was a lot of travel and a whole bunch of entertainment; we were up until all hours of the night. When we were out, he was always around other people from work, and he never stopped talking; he was like the Energizer bunny. He told story after story, and people depended on him to keep the conversation lively.

We also did a lot of entertaining at our house. Our guests were friends he had made, as well as friends I had made, and some of them remain friends to this day. It really was fun, although I always got stuck cleaning it up. Small price to pay, but some yeoman's contributions from David would have been appreciated.

This was our life for the next several years. If he said it once, he said it a million times: We were going to be in

Tennessee five years max. He was doing really well at his job, and I had gotten my master's degree in education. By this time I had gotten a teaching job at a really good independent girls' school, and I loved it.

Clean House

It's one thing to be able to handle change when you see it coming, but when it comes out of the blue, it can really wreak havoc. Suddenly, an international group came in and cleaned house at David's company; that included giving him the heave-ho. We had been in Memphis six or seven years by this time, and, of course, he wasn't counting on getting let go. As the old saying goes, he never saw it coming.

I was fearful of what was coming next, mostly because *I had no clue* what was coming next. One thing I knew was that I didn't want to move again. Anyone who has experienced making a big move anywhere, let alone halfway across the USA, needs something really special in life and a great sense of adventure to come along to inspire them to pick up and move again, even if it's just halfway across town.

Jobless, David spent most of his time at home, networking. Dishes were everywhere, as could be expected. It wasn't a real mess, just a sign of the times; our kitchen was being put to good use, all day, every day.

Eventually, through my teaching job, I found out I had a connection with a major manufacturing company in town. My connection told me to tell my husband to grab his resumé and have him go to company headquarters for some interviews. He ultimately came away with a new job less than a year after being declared a free agent. The new job was maybe a step down from what he had been doing at his old place, but it paid fairly well and kept us safely in the black.

Frequent Fliers

We did a lot of international travel during those years in Tennessee, and that was when some red flags started popping up as well, ones that I chose to ignore—at the time. One trip involved an all-night flight to Germany. Just after we got off the plane upon our arrival there, this buxom blonde walks by. David proceeds to follow her for a few seconds, squeezing both his hands in front of him while mouthing "Mama, Mama." OK, it was all in good fun, but it just wasn't adding up for me. That's when I first realized, or at least remember realizing—there probably had been earlier hints—that his maturity level wasn't matching up to his age (early forties).

The good thing was I was starting to feel more independent; a little voice in the back of my head told me I might someday be needing the confidence and skill to live independently. The busty blonde in Germany was a warning sign. That might be why I was so grateful that I now had a master's degree. On top of that, Mom had found a great job downtown working as a receptionist at a law firm for what turned out to be twenty-six years. Meanwhile, Corrine was establishing herself as a very competent court reporter—she got a job in no time at all, thanks to the guy I had worked for in New Jersey calling his buddy in Memphis and saying, "You need to hire this girl." She went to work right away.

One of the things that allowed my mom and sister to move out of our house quicker was that Corinne was already working and making good money. David, in all this, managed to use Mom's new job as a receptionist to take another dig, saying, "She gives good phone." Another red flag—wiseass humor that steps over the line.

Wedding Belle

Then there was the wedding. Thinking of it brings back a whiff of exhaustion . . . then I cringe. We had been living in Memphis about a year and a half—engaged the whole time; me proudly brandishing my storefront window engagement ring—when we got married in November 1994. We were both Catholic, but because David had already been married once before, and in a Catholic Church, he couldn't do that again. So we got married in a Unitarian Church downtown, right on the Mississippi River.

When Wedding Day came, I was spent, exhausted. David stayed at the house with his family, while I slept on the pullout couch at my mother's place. I didn't sleep well at all the night before, although I don't remember having any bad dreams or nightmares—those would come later, in living, wide-awake color. I had friends in town and a big group of us, including Mom and Corinne, went out to dinner. No wild parties for us.

Before the wedding, I can remember going back to the house to pick up something, and there was a throng of people staying there and not enough towels. David's mom was running around looking for a Sharpie to mark the towels, and I put a halt to that real quick. I told her, "Everyone gets one towel and that's it. We're not going to use Sharpies to mark the towels." Then there was her boyfriend who somehow ended up putting on David's tux pants and coming downstairs and saying, "I can't wear these. They're too short." It was all crazy.

Our wedding was set for late afternoon, 4:00 P.M., on a Friday. The ceremony itself was quite stunning. The seats were like an amphitheater with one whole wall made of glass overlooking the Mississippi River, and everyone there could look outside and see barges going by. As they say, there wasn't a bad seat in the house. A lot of our guests were late getting to the church, as was David. Finding the church wasn't easy, at least not for David. The service started a few minutes late, but that was no big deal.

There were about 125 people there, most from out of town or fellow workers at David's first job in Memphis (this was still several years before the buyout). The ring bearer and flower girl were students of mine from the school at which I taught; a good friend of mine, Nikki from college, did one reading and one of David's good friends did another. When it came time to exchange vows, I belted mine out. I'm not exactly sure why, except I suspect that it was important to me for everyone in the church to hear what I was saying and that I believed in what I was saying.

Added nice touches that day were the boyfriend of my newly minted mother-in-law playing the piano at both the wedding service and the reception; a homemade wedding cake/carrot cake that was amazing and made by his aunt; and an Irish friend (actually from Ireland) of David's reading poetry during the reception dinner with his delightfully authentic Irish brogue.

Ah, yes, the luck of the Irish, and, unbeknownst to me, my luck was starting to run out.

3

Baby, Baby

W E STAYED IN MEMPHIS FOR ABOUT EIGHT YEARS AFTER
WE WERE MARRIED. Like most young women now
brandishing a wedding ring, I was ready to have children.
So was David, as far as I knew.

He settled into his second job in Memphis. By now,
though, he was getting the itch and was ready to move
back to the East Coast. David had stayed in touch with a
good friend of his there who offered him a position at a
company in Manhattan, and David took it.

In spring 2001, he moved back up there and into a
tiny apartment in the Village. All this pleased him to no
end. He was happy to be moving back up there, and he
just loved the sense of adventure that New York City and
the surrounding area gave him. You could tell by how
quickly he talked when he spoke to me. It gave him more
fresh stories to share. Meanwhile, I stayed behind in
Tennessee to finish the school year where I was teaching.

Once the school year was over, I would pack up and move to join him.

There also was the small matter of our wanting to have a baby. And we kept trying. We tried and tried and tried, but it just wasn't happening. I wasn't getting pregnant. I would always wonder if we tried enough times, or if we were trying "hard enough." Who wouldn't?

I finally went looking for help, searching for a doctor, and eventually found one, a fertility specialist. This is while we were still living in Memphis. He suggested we take a conservative approach, starting with a procedure known as intrauterine insemination—IUI, for short. It is a type of artificial insemination that involves a procedure for treating infertility.

As I am writing this, it is with the realization that it has been more than twenty years since I had initiated the IUI procedures. So it shouldn't be a shock to know that I had to do a little research to help explain what I did with the IUI treatments. I found what I was looking for at the Mayo Clinic website, which explains that, using semen provided by the male—David, in my case— sperm is extracted, cleaned, and concentrated before it is placed directly into the woman's uterus. Timing is everything, in that this has to be done as closely as possible to that time of the month when your ovary releases one or more eggs that are then to be fertilized. In other words, your period.[1]

The next step is to cross your fingers and hope—or pray (or do both)—that the sperm will swim into the fallopian tube to fertilize an egg, producing a normal and healthy pregnancy. Depending on the reasons for the woman's infertility, IUI can either be timed to coincide with your normal cycle or helped along with fertility medications.

Although intrauterine insemination is considered fairly simple and relatively safe, the risks include infection, spotting (a small amount of vaginal bleeding), and even multiple pregnancy; the latter risk, however, usually results from an IUI procedure done in conjunction with ovulation-inducing medications.

As for that part about cleaning or "washing" the sperm before it is inserted—such a washing process is needed because there are nonsperm agents in semen that can trigger reactions in the female body that might obstruct fertilization. The washing process is actually a separation process. The highly active, normal sperm is isolated from lower-quality sperm and other unwanted elements, thus enhancing the likelihood of achieving pregnancy.[2]

That's the science behind what I went through as a young woman in her twenties looking to start a family. As you might have guessed, there is no part of the IUI procedure that involves sexual intimacy (aka sexual intercourse) between husband and wife. Certainly not in a doctor's office with the doctor, his nurse, and other assistants always walking around, occasionally checking in to see how things are going.

Trying to Make a Baby

Prior to our moving back to the East Coast, we—or should I say I?—did four of these IUIs. The procedure itself involves threading a tube up through the mommy-wannabe.

The first time I went through a procedure, we ran into an obstacle. Literally. I don't know how this happened, but while the tubing was being threaded upward, it hit somewhere inside of me. Immediately, I was doubled over in cramps, although I managed to get through it. If I remember right, the tubing had a tiny camera on the end of it, so the doctor could see when the tube got to the right spot for the sperm to be released.

Afterward, I remember walking through the Happi-Store, a cute Memphis store, an ironic moment. My pain went unrecognized by David. Emotionally, that's a different story. I went through four IUI procedures between the time we were married and when we picked up and moved back East. It's been a number of years now, and I can't remember a lot of details from that time, only just how profoundly sad I was after none of the procedures worked. I didn't get pregnant.

I had been hesitant to do it again after the failure of the first such procedure, mostly because of the cramping I experienced when the tubing "ran into something" inside of me. The next few times I did it, though, I took some pain pills just in case. These procedures were done at the fertility clinic, and I went through them in pretty rapid succession. I did them all within a period of six months to a year, right up to the time that we moved back to the East Coast.

The folks at the fertility clinic didn't really know what the problem was—why I wasn't getting pregnant. I do remember, though, that at that time they hadn't done any testing of my eggs or anything like that. The only thing they could figure out was that we needed a little assistance.

After I determined that the IUIs weren't going to work for me, we wondered what our next move would be. Adoption came up in conversation every now and then, and at first, David seemed quite willing to go that route.

Once I joined him back East, I somehow felt optimistic about things. The grass looked greener to me. Of course, this grass would need to be fertilized, too. I hadn't given up on trying to get pregnant, and I was excited about having new prospects with new doctors to see what they might be able to do for me (us?). I quickly found a fertility clinic that seemed well suited for me. By this time, I had a new job, teaching first grade. We had moved out of the small apartment in the Village, and we bought a fourth-floor co-op, which was actually a unit in an apartment building, except you own your own unit. What's the difference between a co-op and a condo? Remember, it was originally an apartment, except in buying it now as a co-op you had to be approved by the co-op board.

After some discussion, we decided the next step for me in my quest to get pregnant and have our first child was in vitro fertilization (IVF). I wasn't giving up. New location. New job. New opportunity. The optimist inside me was jumping for joy, even if there wasn't a baby yet—but I believed there soon would be. A fresh start, in all respects.

I never thought for a minute that it would not work. Millions of women have undergone IVF procedures over the years, but for those of you not really familiar with it, let me offer an overview of how IVF works, with thanks once again to my research assistants, the folks at Mayo Clinic who prepare content for their website at mayoclinic.org.

Like IUI, in vitro fertilization (IVF) is a somewhat invasive procedure, as well as a somewhat complex one. Yet it is considered the most effective form of assisted reproductive technology. The main difference between the two is that while the male partner's sperm for IUI is injected into the woman via a tube threaded into the area of her eggs inside her uterus, the IVF procedure involves removing some of the woman's eggs and injecting sperm into them in a laboratory setting.[3]

As explained by Mayo Clinic, during IVF, mature eggs are retrieved from the female's ovaries and removed to a lab where they are then to be fertilized by sperm provided by her male partner. Once the egg (the embryo) or eggs (embryos) are fertilized, they are returned to the uterus. But it doesn't happen all at once. A complete cycle of IVF encompasses about three weeks, although the process can take even longer when these steps are further broken down into different parts.

Now here's where it gets interesting. With IVF, your options are not limited to just the eggs that originate in your own (the woman's) body or the sperm provided by your male partner. The procedure can be carried out by a donor—whether known or anonymous—providing their eggs, sperm, or embryos. Furthermore, there are cases in which it is deemed a better, potentially more-effective option to use a gestational carrier—another woman who has an embryo (the fertilized egg from the laboratory) implanted in her uterus. The wonders of modern-day science.[4]

David and I didn't have a need for any gestational carriers or second-party donors (whether known or unknown to us). Whatever issues we had been having in trying to conceive between the two of us—and this is as good a place as any to say that one thing we did have going for us was still a very active sex life—we were able to provide our own eggs (mine) and our own sperm (his).

For me, life as an IVF patient started out at 5:00 A.M. That's when I would head to the fertility clinic every day to give blood, one or two vials a day. This went on for a week or two. It was about a thirty-minute drive, and I drove myself there and then to school. The purpose was for them to be able check on me, via testing my blood, to see when I was ovulating. After that, at least in my case, came the injections that were intended to increase the number of eggs—hopefully, healthy ones—inside me and therefore boost my chances of getting a healthy embryo that would be inserted back into me.

No appointment was needed each time I went, but I learned quickly that you wanted to be there early because it was first-come, first-served. Even as early as I got there, I usually had to wait a while, but I was always able to get out of there and to school in time for the start of classes.

After I gave blood each time, there was no problem with me leaving the clinic, jumping into the car, and driving myself to school. I wasn't going to faint or anything like that—they made sure of that. That's one of the many great things about the human body; as long as you are taking care of it properly, it can replenish its own blood supply pretty quickly. Otherwise, there's no way I could have gone there every day for ten days over a two-week period and given a vial or two of blood and then left there fit to drive fifteen minutes in the heavy East Coast traffic, no less.

Each day there, I was again another number (a different number each day). The women were lined up, each in her own chair, with her arms constricted by that rubber band, when once released made it easier to withdraw blood. Once they did that, you sat there for a minute, they bandaged you up, and away you went, for me off to school. Someone at the clinic would then call later in the day to let you know if you needed to come back the next day or not.

The injections, each time followed by an ultrasound to see how many eggs I had, I performed myself at home. That also meant going to the local pharmacy—a special drugstore, in fact—to pick up all my medicines. Back at home, I had to measure out and then inject these drugs into my own body, usually a leg or my stomach. The idea was to increase the number of healthy eggs in me and make sure my body had the right amount of progesterone in it to help support the subsequent growth of eggs that would be reinserted following fertilization.

It was a surreal time. I ended up putting myself through four series of IVF treatments, each time making those trips to the pharmacy, then measuring out the shots (usually ten cc's), and giving myself the injections, with no one there to help me—certainly not David. He was too busy. Or something. In fact, I don't remember him being present any of the times I was putting myself through this ritual; he was always at work. OK, he *was* there with me when it came time for me to give myself progesterone shots in my bottom—those he did for me because it wasn't going to work too well with my trying to reach around, holding a needle, and then sticking it into my butt in the right place. That, he took seriously.

Other than those times in which David shot me in the butt, he was not to be seen during those times of self-administering IVF shots. And when he came home at night from work? There wasn't much to discuss about my IVF tribulations and needle pricks. When I started to talk about what I had done that day, he would change the subject and switch gears in the conversation. Whenever we did talk about the IVF stuff, it would always be just a brief interlude to part of another conversation, with him choosing the topic. Not a whole lot of communication or intimacy going on there.

OK, if you're keeping score at home, let me summarize for you how things turned out in "our" attempts for me to get pregnant via IVF and have a baby.

Counting Eggs

The first time we did the IVF procedure, we came up with eight eggs taken out of me with which to work. After those were extracted, they were put into petri dishes to be fertilized with the sperm, and all this was done at the clinic. When they told us there were eight eggs, it was great news! The more healthy eggs I had, the better my chances of getting pregnant. But not all eight successfully "took." The second time I did it, I got four eggs and none of them were subsequently fertilized. The third time I got one and the fourth time none, and that was hugely disappointing.

During all this, they put the fertilized eggs back inside of me, but none of them "took." They are hard to implant. Of the ones they reinserted into me, none of them attached to the womb like they were supposed to. There were lots of drugs involved to help in the process, although no one—including me—knew going in how I would react to them and if they would improve my chances of getting pregnant. I remained hopeful the whole time, but I didn't want to get too excited, either. One thing was, I never really understood why all the eggs that were taken out of me didn't get fertilized, or "take."

I remember in particular the last time that the IVF procedure didn't "take" with me. David and I were on a trip out of town with his father, when I got a phone call telling me that there were no eggs to work with, meaning my chances were officially nil. I just lost it; I was an emotional mess, and for the moment David was not around. We weren't just "out of town," either; we were *waaaayyy* out of town, holed up in a cabin in far north Minnesota, the northernmost point in the United States. We had flown into an airport in Canada because it was the closest large airport to where the cabin was. Even then, it was a four-hour drive to get there.

David's dad had found this place. It was in a nice spot, right on the lake that was a haven for fishermen. This must have been summertime because I wasn't working that month—I've always worked—so I'm assuming this was during my summer break from school. It was a very remote cabin, and as cozy and convenient as it might have been for guys who loved isolation, baiting hooks, and scouring the best lures for catching the biggest fish. I hated that it was so hard to get to. Drive and drive and drive.

At the time I got the phone call, David was off somewhere else; all I knew is he wasn't in the cabin. It was just David's dad and me, and within minutes after I got the bad news on the phone, his dad and I got into a big row. A fight, actually. Lots of yelling. There was zero empathy on his part. Here I was, essentially having an emotional breakdown over some devastating news (in my opinion), and he was so indifferent about all this. Not a whole lot of support for his daughter-in-law at that point, which was par for the course for the entire time that David and I were married.

As soon as David got back to the cabin, I told him about what had happened. He said we were leaving.

Once we had loaded the car, we headed back to the airport and hung out there until it was time for our flight to depart. We had actually planned all along to leave that day, but we departed from the cabin what turned out to be two to three hours early. I just had to get the heck out of Dodge.

You can say all you want about David's father and me being from different generations, and that I needed to understand that he came out of an era in which men were programmed to be macho and tuck their feelings inside, but I didn't accept that as an excuse. If you are human, act like one. For God's sake, your son's wife needs an empathetic ear at a life-changing moment, and the dad, a member of "the Greatest Generation," instead cranks up the curmudgeon act a few decibels, and there is no love to be shown. Not even an attempt at faking it.

Bottom line: my IVF treatments weren't working for me, either—just like what I had gone through with the IUI treatments. I've heard how emotionally ravaging it can be for a woman to lose a baby by miscarriage; I suspect that going through multiple failed attempts at assisted pregnancy has got to rank close to that. Going through multiple IUI attempts followed by a succession of IVF procedures involves a significant investment of time, money, hope, dreams, expectations, and worry, all crunched together on a roller coaster ride that goes on for months, if not years.

So now that the IVFs had failed and I was still going nowhere in "our" quest to have a family—a sentiment that was quickly evolving into a "me" thing vs. an "us" thing— all I could wonder was, "What next?" By this time, David and I still hadn't talked much about what was happening with these failed treatments, what exactly had happened, or what it all meant. At the time, I assumed the problem was his—David's sperm had been tested, and he was told that he had a low sperm count. That's why I pegged his apparent issue as the reason for why we were still babyless. Again, that was never discussed.

Nor did I spend much, if any, time after the IVF failures trying to learn more about the topic—such as how to deal with being childless despite repeated attempts at pregnancy and the emotional fallout, while other female friends my age were popping out babies. My father-in-law didn't want to hear about it, and for the most part I just shut it down after that. In writing this book, I came across an interesting article on huffpost.com (Huffington Post) addressing emotional turmoil resulting from failed IVFs. Following is an excerpt from the 2018 article "IVF Failure Is Devastating and More Common Than You Think," written by clinical psychologist Dr. Elizabeth Merrill:

"The emotional impact of a failed IVF cycle is overwhelming and cannot be overstated," writes Merrill, who says she herself had experienced a time when her IVF treatments failed to "take" despite her using twenty eggs she had had extracted and frozen several years earlier. "Infertile women have been found to have elevated anxiety and depression levels similar to women with heart disease and cancer. To many, infertility means loss—loss of reproductive capacity, loss of a child, loss of genetic continuity, loss of a pregnancy experience, and/or loss of the potential to reproduce biological offspring with an intimate partner. With each failed IVF cycle, my partner and I were forced to grapple with the loss of our fantasy family and a loss of faith in science." [5]

Merrill cites recent statistics from the Centers for Disease Control and Prevention (CDC) that show U.S. fertility clinics performing 231,936 IVF cycles in 2015, with 60,778 of those leading to deliveries. That means that only 26 percent of IVF cycles produce babies, with that percentage dropping significantly after a woman hits the age of forty.[6]

So, it turns out, I had plenty of company in my personal grief, and *grief* is the right word here. There's some consolation there. Merrill adds, "Many couples find themselves in grief or in mourning after a failed IVF cycle. After our first failure, I felt hopeless. I'd assumed I was going to become a mother. When that didn't happen, I felt as if someone close to me had died. After all, IVF was supposed to be a miracle cure, allowing me to pursue my career and ultimately build my family."[7]

Next Stop: Adoption Agency

Sometime over the next several months following the last of my IVF treatments, once I had gathered my wits and regained the motivation for starting a family, we started the process of adoption—or should I say, I started it. David's verbalized approval only came after some discussion between us. Now that I think about it, it was probably already a losing battle in terms of getting his buy-in for adoption.

Once we gave ourselves the green light to adopt, I immediately jumped in to start filling out the scads of paperwork needed for the adoption process—in fact, it was more like tons of paperwork. I'm not sure how much a "scad" weighs, but it can't be as much as a ton. There were lots of questions for which I needed David's help in answering, along with checks to be written and a home visit that would require the both of us, and he did all this willingly.

What I didn't know at the time was that David's heart wasn't in this. He was only along for the ride, and I was out in front wearing a harness, so to speak, dragging him behind me. Yet, I was still clueless.

4

'A' Is for Adoption

WITHOUT LOOKING IT UP, I'M SAFE IN SAYING THAT David and I were not the first married couple to ever disagree on whether or not to adopt a child. It just took us a while to figure out that we were not on the same page. His waning interest in bringing home a child that was not conceived and birthed by us was actually a blinking red light.

Once we finally realized that medically assisted conception and birth wasn't going to work out for us, the next step was adoption. What choice did we have? Is there another option behind the third door, assuming you want to have and raise children as part of a traditional family?

The adoption process begins with—or at least *should* begin with—the assumption that both husband and wife (or however you define your relationship) are in the game together—that they are in agreement they

47

want to do it, and they understand the commitment they are about to make. It also involves confronting and confirming the stark realization that, in many cases, childbearing is no longer in the equation; that by itself can be emotionally trying, to put it mildly. Your life is about to change, and in a manner nothing like what you had anticipated when you were exchanging wedding vows however many years earlier. Welcome to your new life. Paradigm shift time.

While putting together my story, I surfed online to see what I could find in terms of the marriage dynamic, one in which the two spouses were not on equal footing when it comes to adoption. A website I found while doing a keywords search ("adoption," "spouse," "affair," etc.) was American Adoptions, at americanadoptions.com. One of their articles addressed the possible reasons behind why one spouse has cold feet about adoption; it mentioned factors such as withdrawal, denial, anger, etc., on the part of the reluctant spouse. I looked through the article but couldn't find the example where the cold-footed spouse has a secret, hot affair with his mistress for which adopting a child would only mess things up. The closest thing I could find in my search was the mention of how comic actor Kevin Hart had backed out of hosting the 2019 Oscars after admitting he had been having an affair while his wife was pregnant. Well, that's sort of similar, right? I was carrying around the expectation of having a child, even if I was not carrying the child myself.

The way I saw it, our adoption process began when we both expressed a serious interest in adoption, and that's not me putting words into David's mouth. I got things started by calling an adoption agency. They might have been referred to me by my fertility clinic; it doesn't matter. I called them up, told them my husband and I were interested in adopting a baby. They mailed us the paperwork to get started, we filled it out, and we were on our way.

Actually, I filled out most of the paperwork, answering most of the questions myself, although there were some that David and I sat down and answered together—some collaboration was required on some questions. The rest I filled out myself. Following are several of the questions from the adoption paperwork:

- How well do you understand the adoption process?
- What are your hopes for your child?
- What do you know about some of the unique challenges faced by children who are adopted?

Then came a home visit from a representative of the adoption agency for a sit-down, two-way interview. This was the first time that I fully realized what we were about to do, and it scared me. It meant coming to grips and accepting that we probably weren't going to have any children of our own. Part of me was thinking we could still do this naturally, although we'd been married nine or ten years and still no children. But I was only thirty-five or thirty-six years old; I was still plenty young enough to have a child, or even several, before the ticking of my biological clock would start pounding in my head.

One thing that disturbed me during that home visit and the questioning was that David and I were given plenty of openings to ask our own questions about how all this would work. Instead, there were just crickets at times. My chatty cutup of a husband, the life of the party and a master storyteller who kept audiences riveted, was sitting there not saying much, which fed into the fear I was feeling. Not a sense of doom, actually, but more a growing sense of doubt that was gaining momentum and picking up speed all the way from my gut to the top of my chestnut-brown-haired head. *This guy is really starting to come across as a son of a bitch.*

Speak up, man! Get together with me on this! Man up!

As the doubt started spreading outward to all regions of my body and brain—keep in mind, we're just getting started in this adoption process; no heavy lifting yet—and while the agency rep was talking and then listening, I was asking myself, *Am I doing this for me alone?* And then I would shift gears, rationalizing; *Ehhh, this is par for the course for David. He never really involves himself in anything deeply—except for work.*

I definitely, if not desperately, wanted a child. I knew he did as well, or at least he had expressed so. Adoption was the next logical step for us, and I knew I would be a good mom.

Westward Ho!

With the adoption process underway, David got around to telling me we were moving to the West Coast. Before that,

50

though, we lived in that little co-op for about a year and a half. We then bought and moved into a brownstone about five to ten miles farther out of the city, accessible by mass transit. All told, we spent about five years living back East. I was teaching the whole time, and he was still working in New York City. Work was good for him, and he was a real climber in the business world—he had always been that way. Along with that, he was really good about maintaining business relationships with friends all over. He had them in Europe, Milwaukee, New York, California, Memphis, elsewhere in the Midwest. You name the place, he probably had a network buddy or two there as well. I sometimes wonder if he had other girls in other ports as well.

Lo and behold, a friend of his in California told him about a job out there and encouraged David to give it a shot, and that's exactly what he did. He went through a big, drawn-out interview process. That included them flying him out there several times to make sure he was right for the job and so he could thoroughly check them out as well. The interview process was a two-way street, of course, although there was no way he was going to turn it down if they offered—and if the dollars and bennies were right. Turns out, they were. He was easy; this was a move he really wanted.

Fortunately, we weren't yet too deep into the adoption process, just barely out of the starting blocks. I contacted the agency we had been using to tell them we were planning to move. In turn they told me that all of the information that had so far been put together could be transferred to an adoption agency in California. That was a relief to me because I had feared that we would have to start the process all over again from the beginning.

The new job on the West Coast was a great job for David because it was the kind of work that he totally knew, and he was thrilled. It was a sweet deal and a terrific position that had just been vacated by a gentleman who was retiring. Still, as good a fit as the job was for him, there was already a lot of work there waiting for him on his plate and he had to get out there, although I couldn't go with him yet. I had to finish out the school year in Summit, New Jersey. So when he moved out West, I was left behind in the brownstone. I finished out the school year, which entailed just a couple more months, and I stayed behind a few more months on top of that, finally moving out there in the early fall.

Later, after David had admitted to the affair, I learned that he had met the woman who would become his girlfriend/mistress while we were still in New Jersey. I hadn't been suspicious at the time, but he had been going out a lot, mostly Wednesday and Thursday nights. I was teaching fifth grade, which took a lot out of me, and I would come home exhausted at the end of the day, which is why I wasn't going out with him. It would be just him going out and meeting up with some buddies, including, as I would find out eventually, one girl buddy-buddy in particular.

David would come home, usually after midnight, pretty much blasted, and this was all during the time after he had met Avery. It had never dawned on me to go out and party on a Wednesday or Thursday night. He asked me once or twice to go with him, but I'm pretty sure he was just going through the motions knowing that I would turn him down. The worst that could have happened was that I would accept and go with him. Then he could have easily whipped out his Plan B, called his pals to ask for a rain check, and taken me some place he knew I liked. That way, he could still get toasted and salvage some fun for the night while checking the box on his to-do list that had my name beside it. Not exactly a win-win in his book, nor in mine, but good enough for each of us in our own way to still feel pretty good about things.

The part about his going out and meeting up with friends—that part was true. David was having a good ol' time, including getting in some male bonding. There were ten brownstones where we lived, which is how David met Derek. This guy was always going out, not doing anything good but drinking, partying, and catting around, on the prowl, occasionally getting into trouble.

One time, Derek and his wife hosted a Saint Patrick's Day party at their house, but I didn't go. That's probably because I was tired (same old story) and had some school-work to do (another same old story). Yes, it's true—I didn't have my Irish on that night.

I think this is where David met Avery. I distinctively remember those events happening right around the same time that I wanted to start telling everyone at school that I wouldn't be coming back the next year, that my husband and I were moving to northern California. I wanted to give them as much advance notice as I could so they would have plenty of time to hire my replacement. On top of that, I was excited to be starting a new adventure and wanted to share the good news with everyone I knew. One problem: David would not let me tell anyone, and I couldn't understand why. At the time, though, it made sense to me that he didn't want to cut all ties only for his new job to not work out and him have to drag himself back to New Jersey a "failure." Which wouldn't have been all that bad; he was much better connected in the New Jersey-New York area than he was out West and could probably rustle up another good job fairly quickly, if he had to.

Once David took the job and moved to California, the adoption thing was put on hold for us—transition time for us; no room to squeeze in adoption proceedings. Once we were both in California and living together in the apartment, I realized just how tiny it was—even with just the two of us and my beautiful West Highland White Terriers. And, once again, he was working all the time— with worlds to conquer and money to make so he could support an all-in girlfriend, while screwing her as well as me, without arousing my suspicions. Yet.

David's new job was with a family-owned company, and he wasn't traveling as much as he had in his previous jobs. There were, however, occasional trips to Europe, because part of his job was helping to grow business relationships internationally. It wasn't long before I was feeling really alone, wondering, *Where am I?* and *What is happening here?* It was just me and the two dogs, and plenty of glasses of wine. David was definitely becoming more detached from me, and for me it was severe loneliness. It's strange to say this, or maybe not, but I was feeling more alone when around him than when I was just by myself.

Eastward Bound

While this—whatever it was—was going on, David was still serving on the board of his former company back in New York City. It wasn't uncommon for him to fly back East on a Thursday or Friday and come back Sunday night. As he was getting ready to leave on those occasions, he would say something like, "I've got another board meeting to go to, and while I'm up there I'm going to go check on the brownstone, too." And I thought that was perfectly normal. I just assumed that we were headed to a point in our marriage that once the brownstone was sold, he would be spending more time with me in California, doing some of the same things we had been doing in years past, when we would go out together and have fun.

After about two months in the microscopic apartment, we started house hunting, looking at different neighborhoods. We were impressed by how pretty everything was. Ultimately, he got a tip on a house, and once I saw it, I remember telling him this will be the most beautiful neighborhood that we will ever live in. It was right off of a Hollywood set; not a blade of grass out of place, and just outside Sacramento.

So there it was; this big, beautiful home . . . and then it became, *What are we going to do about it?* Even when we got into our new house, though, he was still traveling back East. The brownstone had been sold, but he would mention something about there still being some paper-work to be done or that he was going to check in with Derek about some things. There was one month in which he went back every weekend, literally.

You know the story, but it bears repeating: It never dawned on me what was really going on. My sister Co-rinne would mention something along those lines to me, and I would just tell her, "There's no way." I never thought there would ever be anyone stupid enough to get involved with him. Nor did I believe he would ever be foolish enough to not only start but also maintain something with someone else while we were married and with a move ac-ross the country. That kind of stuff just never crossed my mind. It was too big!

Everything seemed to be intact with us—when he was home we were together in every sense of the word—and we were taking trips all over the place. It was him, me, and my loneliness. Cape Cod. Hilton Head. London. Plus I was getting to know all the people in his new California-based business. It was a great company, wonderful people. I re-member telling him how not only was it a family-owned company, but it truly was a family of its own.

I reminded him of this later after I found out he was having the affair, saying to him that, "I will tell everybody here what you have done." Now that would have gone over really well. People who are part of committed families don't do that sort of thing, especially when they are in the process of adoption.

Once we got settled into the new house, I contacted an adoption agency a few hours south of Sacramento.

They sent the paperwork we needed, and we sent a check in as initial payment, as required. Actually, I wrote the check out of my own account, even though I wasn't working at the time. I hadn't been looking, although I intended to get another teaching job. I had joined him there in November, and now it was January or February, so, essentially, I was taking a year off from work as there weren't many schools in a position to hire a full-time teacher in the middle of the school year.

About that time, David had another business trip coming up. It was one where we would drive eight hours to Palm Springs in order for him to earn some continuing-education credits to stay current in his field. It worked out that the adoption agency was along the way. We built in some time on the trip so we could stop there and touch base with whom we needed to be in contact. That's when and where the second red flag went up in our attempt to adopt, and it wasn't the agency that waved the red flag; it was David. The truth of his intent in terms of where we were headed as a family (nowhere, it turns out) was starting to seep out, and it was miserable to experience.

Scrooge's Emergence

David was horrible once we got to the agency and started talking to the agency people. He was asking questions that were couched in language critiquing the process—and not in a good way. He was being cynical about the whole thing. It sounded an awful lot like he was building a case as to why we should ditch this adoption agency. All I could think while he was grilling them, besides feeling embarrassment and shock, was that he was becoming this grumpy old man, a curmudgeon. It was disgraceful. I would soon realize, though, that it was clear he didn't want to adopt, regardless what adoption agency we talked to.

Before we went on this trip, I had bought a photo album at the advice of the agency. They had told me that starting a "birth album" would be good not only for us, but also for our adopted child as he or she grew up. The suggestion was to establish a timeline that would strengthen his or her bonds with not just David and me, but with our families as a whole.

I loved the idea. It wasn't just for us or our child-to-be, either—it was also for the benefit of the prospective birth mothers. It was a cute, handy way to 'sell' them on our worthiness and suitability for raising a child.

I went to a stationery store to pick out an album and then went home. My next task was to gather photos of Dad and me as well as our respective families to put in the album. It was also suggested to us that we put clippings and letters in the album—anything appropriate to flesh out our story and paint us as real people ready to raise and love a child.

Whatever ended up in the album would also help tell our story of how we had attempted for years to have a child of our own, including medically assisted pregnancy, without success. There was nothing impulsive about what we were doing, and we (I) had already suffered enough through the failed IUIs and IVFs. That had to count for something.

I ended up with about twenty to twenty-five pages of photos in the album, which had a yellowish-greenish cover—I had tried to choose neutral colors. I retrieved some photos from different times in our marriage, such as some of us dressed up at Christmas, standing in front of the tree, but realized we still didn't have as many photos suitable for the album as I would have liked. There was more work to be done with clippings and anything else I could think of to help tell our story.

What I didn't count on was David's attitude and behavior at the adoption agency when we stopped there en route to Palm Springs. Totally uncalled for. It was a terrible meeting—all David's fault. Consequently, our time at the final destination where he was to earn those education credits was a mess. We still had the other half of our drive of three and a half hours to get from the agency to where he needed to be. As we were driving, I tried to initiate discussion about the adoption agency, but he just kept poking holes in my balloons.

Not long after we got back home, David's mom and aunt came to visit, as did his uncle and his uncle's wife. They all wanted to come see our new home. It was the four of them driving the whole way from the Midwest.

Walking the Dogs

A few hours after they arrived, it was time for me to take the dogs out for a walk. David asked if he could come along, which is something that he had rarely done, if at all (I couldn't remember such an occurrence.). In any event, I was surprised . . . and it aroused suspicion in me. It was during that walk that he told me he didn't want to adopt. I was blown away. I was very upset, but punching his lights out was out of the question, so in my indignation, I said to him, "What are we going to do? You have ruined my life! Why have we done all this work back in New Jersey and then here to adopt?" And he said, "Hey, it was all you and not me."

Where's a punching bag, or an Uzi, when you need one?

I was hysterical, and when we got back into the house, I calmed down and went and told his mother. I liked her and knew that I could talk to her. I also remember thinking, *What a jerk, what a coward, using the occasion of his mother visiting us, and right after she had arrived, to tell me that he didn't want to adopt.* I knew I couldn't get *too* upset and make a huge scene. Of course, there had been so much pushback from him during that stopover at the adoption agency that I should have known then and there that he simply didn't want to adopt. That bit of denial was on me.

Back in New Jersey, he had helped in the adoption process, at least in terms of sitting in for the interview process with the agency rep and filling out paperwork with me. As for what happened during our stop at the adoption agency on the West Coast, I chalked it up to his being under some sort of work-related stress. As much of a horror story as that was, I never thought about cutting off any of the emotional, sexual stuff between us. Maybe I saw that as the gateway for staying together—perhaps it was me doing my duty as a wife, as old-fashioned as that sounds. Nowadays, it would be different.

David was a master at keeping me there, not bucking him, always looking forward to the next thing, stringing me along. He was always dangling something in front of me, like another trip that was coming up, or "We're going to take so-and-so out to dinner next week," or discussing when we would next go to see his mother because he knew I liked her. He was a puppet master, and I was the puppet.

What he couldn't have known was that his days of dangling a carrot in front of me, and me going for the bait, were about to come to an end. I was waking up to life.

5

'A' Is Also
for Adultery

A COULD ALSO STAND FOR AFFAIR OR EVEN AUTOPSY. Or Asshole, and don't even let me get started in the Bs. Any one of those first three 'A's' is as fitting as either of the other two. David was the asshole who had the affair. Picking through the pieces from our sham marriage was my version of an autopsy, I suppose.

What had gone on with us back at the house with his mom et al there, following our trip, had created a massive amount of confusion for me. That's not all that was going on inside my head. Yet we could not really talk about it because his family was there for a few more days, and so that was a lot of simmer time—not to be confused with summertime. We had to discuss this further, but we couldn't. And some of his family being there was his cover.

Those thirty days between David's no-adoption declaration and my back-door confrontation with him were excruciating . . . for me. Not so much for David; it was more like a speed bump for him. He still had his work and a lot of solo travel to keep him occupied, so I was stuck alone at home with nothing to do but process the loss of a child from an adoption that never made it to the finish line. Nothing had come out of this except that he didn't want to adopt.

For the first time in our twelve years of marriage, it felt like my life was making a turn and sailing on a different course. There was no one else on the boat to help me jibe or scull. I kept asking myself, *Why are we here, and what are we doing here? I don't really know anybody out here; I have no friends here.* I just had the two dogs, and David was traveling the whole time, having a good ol' time—even better, it turns out, than I had originally suspected.

Then it finally hit me that morning crawling out of bed, when I went to him and asked him, "Are you having an affair?"

That same day I told several neighbors, one of whom gave me the name of the therapist that her son had seen for some sort of issue. I went back into my house, went straight to the phone and, as I touched on earlier, called the therapist, but she told me she didn't have any openings. But I didn't hang up. The good news was that I was talking to her and not some gatekeeper assistant who probably would have tried to shoo me away at that point.

I was feeling extremely unempowered at that point and told my therapist about it. As soon as I said that word ('unempowered'), she said, "Hold it. Let me check my appointment book." When she came back, she told me that she could see me that afternoon. I never really understood that, where in one breath she told me she had no spots available and then in the next she had space for me. But I wasn't going to question it.

One Long Root Canal

Considering the state of mind I was in, trying to reach deep to get beyond the blur, my situation was like the person who calls the dentist with a toothache, knowing they will probably need a root canal. Well, it was an emergency for me, and I needed that root canal, and I needed it right then!

When I got there and walked into the therapist's office, it struck me how businesslike it was there. An assistant greeted me and handed me some paperwork to fill out, and I did all that as best I could. It was hard because I was still in shock. The stuff I had to fill out was pretty basic, which is good, because I was in no shape to dig into answering a bunch of tough, prying questions. One form asked me to summarize what was going on in my relationship with my spouse. It also included a part asking me how I was going to pay for the therapy.

The therapist ended up seeing me for about an hour, and she was brutal—but she was good. She got right to the heart of the matter, and I walked out of there amazed. Going into her counseling room, I thought the whole thing was going to be about why *he* would do this, but her focus was more on me. I wasn't prepared for that. *I hadn't done anything wrong. Why are you grilling me?* I mean, *What the hell?!*

65

This was probably the first time in my life that I was starting to really think about who I was and who I had become through twelve years of marriage. At first I was thinking, *Why are we even doing this session this way? **He did it!*** But my therapist stayed calm and businesslike with me—persistent, but speaking clearly and listening intently. I needed that, even though part of me inside was still bucking at the exchange. She said, "You're fine. Get it together."

Later on, when David accompanied me to the therapist, there would be times when it was my turn to talk and I would get so upset, raising my voice and/or crying, and she would tell him, "Leave her alone; let her get through it herself." That's because he would sometimes try to butt in, being his usual calm Zen self, trying to speak for the both of us. She would essentially shush him up, saying we were talking about me. I liked that, how she managed the counseling sessions with both him and me in the room.

Rachel A and Rachel B

My first day at the therapist's office, when it was still just me there, I was introduced to a concept known as Rachel A and Rachel B. (Just as a reminder, Rachel is not my real name. It is one of many that have been changed in this book.) Rachel A was the side of me that kept hanging on to things and letting them fester. In that regard I was really good at shocking myself, such as replaying flashbacks in my mind and thinking about them over and over. Most people know this as being stuck in the past, and letting it wash over you, again and again. The other me, Rachel B, was always trying to move forward without being tied to the past. I was going in two different directions at once.

Early on in the counseling process, the task was to get Rachel A and Rachel B in sync with one another. It was kind of weird at first, sounding like a bunch of psychobabble nonsense meant for someone with real problems—certainly not me. I had a lot to learn about myself obviously. My therapist was using this tactic to try to help each of us out—Rachel A and Rachel B—and soon I found it fascinating.

I learned some amazing things in that first session, like all kinds of new data and statistics. Yet my therapist was cramming my brain with stuff. I was not taking notes, though. I was sobbing—no way for me to take notes at the time. After a while, none of this was getting through. It was me just sitting there listening to her. Things were just flying at me and bouncing off, nothing penetrating the exterior of my jam-packed interior. Things were either flying by me or bouncing off of me.

I didn't know where all this was leading, and I didn't know where all this was going, either. I was feeling even more pain at this time—emotional pain. The hardest part in all this was trying to figure it out—what had happened and what the triggers had been. Then there was the anxiety I was experiencing, wave after wave. Plus lack of sleep. It was going to be a lot of hard work, and a whole lot of questions. All that was packed into the first day of counseling, and it lasted about an hour and a half.

There's no question that I was raw—raw emotionally

and raw in other areas of my life that could be defined. Here is what I wrote in my journal during that week, ten years ago:

> This was the beginning of a very damaging phase to myself. I demanded every detail of the relationship which led me to become beside myself, devastated. My anger could be described by feeling out of control, anxious, and with bouts of needing to flee California and then needing to see my husband. My anger ripped away at my stomach and my throat as if hot coffee were being poured into me constantly.

> So here begins a series of therapy sessions, where I learned and continued to demand too much hurtful information as well as ways to cope. But my mind was like a funnel with the narrow end closed off. Only the shocking details would be allowed in my mind. (These) details were forming one of the best romance movies of the century, a blockbuster hit that didn't include me. I ignored my own thoughts and needs.

> I seem to know what the right choices are, but it takes my heart a while to catch up with my brain. Throughout this ordeal, I have gained some confidence and strength, but I still ponder the question, Why is it so easy for me to avoid getting to know me?

> I have been given gifts—gifts of truth, peace, and time. As with any gifts, they are meant to be nurtured and tended to. I plan to continue doing the hard work.

'You Need That'

At my therapist's request, I was accompanied by David on the next visit, which took place the following week. I don't think he had a huge problem with it; he went with me to the session, right? The biggest motivation getting him to go was his seeing how upset I was when he got home that first night. After I told him that I had been to counseling that afternoon, he said, "That's good. You need that."

What he was saying to me, in so many words, was, "I'm so glad that you did that for yourself." He was so condescending. I'm thinking, *You have a problem. You are having an affair, and not only that, but you've been having an affair while we were talking about adopting.* The whole thing to me was just preposterous. Here he was allegedly worried about *me,* when I knew that we had so many things to work out; those things involved him just as much as they involved me. This was David just being David, consistent with his behavior and crappy attitude toward me dating back several years. Getting him to admit that *he* needed help was going to be a chore, one well above my pay grade.

That first night after he got home, he also wanted to know how I had found a therapist so fast. I told him about the referral that I had gotten from a neighbor—that she had given me the name of a therapist. What's strange is that he didn't ask me anything about what I had discussed with the therapist, or even which neighbor I had talked to. Just like everything else, he was so much about himself.

Even that night, he was changing the subject to what time he had to be at work that next day, things that he was having to do, and all the work-related travel that he had coming up soon.

At the time we talked, I had forgotten that I had booked a flight in the next couple days to go to Tennessee to visit my mom and Corinne. I left a few days later for that trip, and I think he left a day after I did for another one of his business trips. He said he had some business to take care of on the East Coast, but I knew he was going to see Avery as well.

I stayed with Corinne while I was in Tennessee. David called me on my cell phone a couple of times while he was traveling. He also called me a couple times after he got back home to our house in California.

To be honest, thinking back, I'm not sure if David and I went to counseling together for the first time before we took our respective simultaneous trips, or if it was after we had both gotten back home. What I do remember is that the first time he and I went to counseling together, he asked the therapist if she thought we had a firm-enough foundation on which we could move forward in our marriage. I took for granted that he already had the answer to this question. I was blown away by that. Even in all my lingering shock and anxiety from learning of his affair, I sure didn't see that coming. At that point, I was still thinking that this had just been a fling between him and this other woman, and that he and I were going to work through this and remain a married couple until one of us passed away.

Things had suddenly reached a whole different depth, and now we had yet another setback on our hands. I was shocked—*This is bigger than I had even imagined*, and at the time I was thinking, *How can this get any worse?* Well, it just had.

During our joint-counseling sessions, we both sat on a comfortable sofa, about a foot apart from each other, and looking only at Melanie, the therapist, the whole time, and not at each other. Well, maybe there were a few quick glances here and there, but nothing significant in terms of eye contact, making faces at one another, me sticking out my tongue at him, or anything like that. It was clear, though, that he didn't want to be there, and he didn't seem to think there was any problem—except, of course, whatever problems I was dealing with. The schmuck. He always acted that way, as if to say with pure arrogance and denial, *I'm good; she's not, obviously*. He didn't have to actually speak it to say it.

Just for the record, some years earlier, back in the 1990s, there had been one other time when he and I had gone to counseling together. That was back when we were living in Tennessee, during that time that my mom and sister had come to stay with us while my mom looked at homes for sale before eventually finding a place for her and my sister. David's expressed concern at that time, and the main reason for that particular counseling session, was his belief that my mom and sister were being too involved in our lives. Or so he thought.

Back then, the first thing David asked the marriage therapist in our first session together was, "When are we going to bring out the hand puppets?" That was his idea of therapy. The therapist just ignored the comment; glossed right over it. At that, David settled into the session and listened. She proceeded to do most of the talking, speaking to both of us at the same time.

As I write this, I can't remember many of the specifics about what my California therapist talked about later, during our counseling after his affair came to light—keep in mind, it's been more than ten years. But I did manage to write down many of the essentials about what was said during those sessions, writing in my journal. Here's some of what I wrote, written when my emotions were still raw and without intent at the time to write a book, so you will see that my writing was about as rough as my emotions:

May 2007:
Marriage therapy has been an excellent outlet for honest communication. I have been and felt lost and lonely and completely forgotten for about a year.

When I misinterpret or jump to conclusions, I need to work on that. When David told me about the affair after I really pushed the issue, he also offered me a sum of money and told me he would take care of me. I understood him to say that he wanted me to leave.

My therapist said that David was guarded and felt that he failed himself, me, and our marriage, and he had trouble facing it.

I heard David say, when asked, that I needed to be with family and I should leave to see M (Mom) and C (Corinne) I thought he was thinking of himself and not me. Halfway there (on my trip to see my mom and sister), I felt good about leaving and that David had my best interests in mind for both of us. Meanwhile, they spent the night together in New Jersey while I was away, and he told her he loved her.

It hurts me tremendously to hear David ask the question, "Do we have a foundation on which to build our marriage or go on from here?" I took for granted that he was happy. David probably won't show remorse, especially after I forced him to come clean, until he is ready.

He is thankful that we have begun counseling and has said that he knows he loves me because it hurts him to see me cry.

According to my therapist, we don't know or understand or hear each other very well. I feel like I hear David asking, "How much effort do I have to put into the marriage in order to go forward?" My therapist says he did not say that and has not heard him say this. My instincts tell me I'm correct.

I feel disconnected from him. I feel like I come third or fourth; not sure I can live like this.

David is working on health, guilt, and defensive guarded issues. I'm traumatized.

I love David and would have trouble not being with him permanently, but is this the right decision, staying? Am I strong or smart enough to do what is right for me? Have I been relying on others to achieve this?

At first I (felt) bad about telling our neighbors, but then remembered I was lost, vulnerable, and angry. David made that choice.

I need to know the full story with my therapist in therapy. Given the importance of David's job, money, stature, progress, and growth, what was he thinking? This is information that could jeopardize his career.

My therapist has explained a reason why David had the affair. He felt powerless with me, as he felt he was unable to have a family. I feel an enormous amount of distrust toward him. It helps to know that we will be honest, totally honest, in our sessions.

I feel angry when he caters to everyone else since I don't feel like I have what I need—a connection, love, a feeling of being loved and needed and abandonment, and a child.

My therapist is shocked that we did not have therapy after our last IVF cycle in the summer of 2005.

I feel that finally having the problems revealed has slowed life down. I have trouble dealing with David, his roving eye, even after the affair.

How does a sensible, logical guy like David lust or sleep with or fall for girls? Because they pay attention to him? I do not feel validated, respected, loved, or special. I wanted to be in a relationship with someone who truly shows that he loves me and wants to be with me. Why does David love me? When I hear David ask me not to use the word *fuck* to describe what he did, I hear that he has feelings for her and wouldn't describe it this way.

Going forward, when I hear him tell a lie, twist the truth, or manipulate a situation, I will be fearful that he will do it to me, too. This I cannot handle. I feel completely empty.

74

As I land in Tennessee, there's a rainbow in the sky. David says, "You love Memphis," and I say, "Well, it feels good here." I hear him say, "You should be there."

I feel afraid to go back to California and afraid to begin a new life in Tennessee. I feel extremely angry and distrust him, rightfully so, as he flies off to the East Coast. I feel pressure and stress to make decisions, and then again, I have to keep telling myself, *No decisions now.*

So what I need are no more secrets and to take the business out of our marriage. Talk to me about what is going on in your head, worry less about money and future and more about today. You can make me feel more important to you by coming home earlier for dinner most nights, initiating physical contact, and planning fun things on the weekends.

It's disturbing to me to hear David always talking about how he's getting older. He does not empathize with my pain. He does not appreciate my point of view. We do not play on a level field. There should be no hierarchy.

We have a serious philosophical difference here. I want him to be with me at parties and dinners, etc. I would like him to share a life with me, not act above me or tell me what to do. Stop overscheduling us.

What I remember most about the counseling time with my therapist is being blown away by all of what was coming out of all this. I was overwhelmed, lost, vulnerable, angry, and feeling just so weak. I hated what the affair was doing to me and my mind, and, as I would eventually find out, it was still going on.

I knew there was so much he wasn't telling me about her. He admitted to the affair and threw some bones out here and there to try to convince me he was being transparent, but he wasn't exactly a tell-all book when it came to his "confiding" in me. He was leaving out a lot of the details while admitting things, and my imagination had no problem filling in the blanks.

Melanie, the therapist, also discussed with me concepts such as low-cost behaviors for me, high-cost behaviors for me, realizations on my part, and so forth. At times I felt like I was a student back in college, sitting in a classroom with notebook open as the professor performs a brain dump on his students. They in turn can barely keep up writing everything down—a challenge even for students who use a laptop. The clutter packed inside my head and the many sobs pouring out made it clear this was a challenge I was having a hard time handling. So here, now, I'm doing my best to remember the outline and highlights of what we discussed and what she gave me for a takeaway.

When David was there with me for sessions, I felt like I heard him asking how much effort he was going to have to put into the marriage going forward. That's what I was reading between the lines even if that wasn't what he was saying verbatim. As good a work ethic as David had for his job, it was hands off for him when it came to dealing with domestic issues, unless, of course, he wanted sex, which at times included me. But working on a marriage, or working to heal a broken one, was beyond his DNA. Some of the difficult work for me included working on my own essential needs. The same would likely hold true for you in the aftermath of a spouse's affair: to feel loved, valued, respected, comfortable, learning how to trust your own body.

As my therapy continued, the therapist gave me ways to move forward—things to observe in him when we were together. I could not process his words, but I learned that when David looked up to the right, it meant that he was telling the truth. Looking sideways meant he was looking for auditory cues, and looking down meant he was trying to access his feelings. I learned that if I had not confronted him about an affair, he would have thought I didn't love him. Probably the most difficult part of our sessions when together was that she told him to stop accommodating and appeasing me. This was mind-blowing because at the time I needed real conversation between us and, sometimes, it began with sobbing tears.

Writing as Catharsis

During that trip I took to Memphis to spend a few days with my mom and sister, following *the* confrontation with David at the back door, I spent gobs of time alone, much of it journaling. Writing all this down was not only cathartic for me, it allowed me ample introspection and a chance to put into words many of the thoughts that were banging around inside my head—to make sense of things.

I highly recommend journaling with honesty and clarity for anyone who has just discovered that his or her spouse has had an affair. It's the No. 1 thing to do, right next to therapy with a skilled therapist. I had access to both. Here's some of what I wrote while staying with my sister in Memphis. Keep in mind, much of what I wrote here was inspired by my first therapy session, even though I was not prompted to write down these sorts of things by my therapist. But they are in keeping with what was discussed between us:

> David does not hear me or empathize with my pain. He is emotionally unavailable, self-absorbed.
>
> In order for a relationship to survive, there must be a spirit of equity and reciprocity. How can you contribute to this?
>
> Hiding or softening the truth paints you as controlling or deceptive.
>
> Then came my questions about the affair:

- How did it begin?
- Is it over?
- Was it all for fun, or at any point did you consider leaving?
- What was the content of your e-mails?
- What attracted you to her?
- I feel hurt that you may have exposed me to diseases.
- Have you ever been with a prostitute or any other woman during our marriage?
- What is missing in this relationship for you?
- Why did you have an affair?

- Tell me about coffee with her in New Jersey.

- Did you take any trips together?

- Who initiated the majority of communication?

- Who initiated sex?

- Talk to me about the pool party when you fell asleep, the Florida hotel room, the canceled meeting in New Jersey.

- If you want our marriage to work, why?

- In your eyes, has our relationship improved since we have been in California? (And he replied, "Yes, with some steps back.")

- Why do you love me?

- What did you fight about?

- What happened when she saw your ring?

- Could she make our lives difficult if she wanted to?

- Is there any other information that would be hurtful to me later on when told to me that you have not yet revealed?

A True Picture

I know I'm throwing a lot at readers in listing all these thoughts and questions, but I share these to offer a true picture of what I went through and how I handled things. Maybe these can help you if you find yourself in a situation similar to mine. Or maybe you have already been there? Consider all this a primer to keep at your side to pull out in a time of need.

Soon after I completed this list of questions and probing statements (actually, I didn't include all of them as written in my journals, but I wanted to provide a good sampling without going too far), I made a list of low-cost behaviors that I wanted to see from David going forward in our marriage post-affair. As you will eventually read in here, none of these ever gained much traction in terms of rehabilitating our marriage.

Here are some of those low-cost behaviors for him I wrote down—a "wish list," if you will, at the time hoping that our marriage was salvageable:

- Limit overnight travel, and invite me to all East Coast trips.
- Tell me if you hear from or see an old friend.
- Tell me when you feel proud of me and why.
- Spend more time in foreplay, kissing, and touching.
- Focus on what I'm saying.
- Be available when I feel lonely or insecure.
- Don't exhale loudly.
- Show affection outside the bedroom.

- When we go out together, show affection and touch base with me frequently. Put your arm around me or hold my hand.
- Show me/copy all paperwork showing my name on everything.
- Your roving eye is hurtful. Mention if you find someone pretty. Don't be sneaky or test the waters to see if they look back at you.
- Listen. Don't necessarily talk all the time.
- Now that we have a permanent residence in California, move bills and mail to our home and not have them mailed to your office.
- Make family calls from home.

For good measure, here are some high-cost behaviors meant for my husband that I would have liked to have seen from him, which I also wrote in my journal more than ten years ago:

- Show me your phone bills and allow me to view your e-mails by giving me your password, with my word that I would never e-mail anyone.
- Answer all my questions about your lover, lies, deceit in front of a therapist so I'm more certain that you are telling the truth.
- Let's take a vacation together this summer.
- Upgrade engagement ring.
- See a female lawyer together to make sure that all my rights are protected.

During those days that I spent at my sister's and away from David, I came to realize how distant we had become.

81

He was no longer paying attention to my feelings; then again, that had never been a strong suit of his in the first place. He was treating me like I was an employee of his or, at best, a roommate.

There was more work ahead of me, and soon it would involve lawyers.

6

Reconciliation: Failure to Launch

ACTUALLY, I PROBABLY SHOULD CALL THIS A HALF-ASSED FAILED ATTEMPT AT RECONCILIATION, because only one of us really made a go of it.

I didn't think I thought it through at the time, but as I write this ten years after all this crap came raining down on me, I now see that there were two separate avenues leading to our divorce. It took my getting to the point where I was detached from all this—finally with a firm grasp of an omniscient view looking back—so that I could see how things had actually been before I knew about his affair. One of those avenues was the old standby, "irreconcilable differences," so often cited by divorcing couples. The other was the highway to hell of his "marital misconduct" which typically, and in my case, refers to a spouse who is screwing around, or, as they say for younger audiences, "having an affair."

I hit the daily double with David. I had it coming from both ends; excuse the yucky pun, but it has some merit to it. Being married to this guy was, for the last several years of our marriage, a really bad case of proverbial flu for me. It took the reality of his affair that was really happening to jolt me to my senses and quickly realize that for the preceding four or five years he had been consistently disrespectful and dismissive of me. Seriously, what had I ever done to him or against him? Yeah, to borrow and tweak a Tina Turner phrase: What did love have to do with it?

Between the time I went to visit my sister and mom in the wake of finding out about his affair, we did make an attempt at reconciliation, or at least I did. David did some of the right things at first after we had met together with the therapist, like going to church with me, and even going to another couple of counseling sessions, but this cat wasn't through prowling around with his girlfriend. It just took me a bit more to find that out, too. But it's not like I didn't have my ear to the ground and my eyes on full alert.

OK, so we did go to church—we were practicing Catholics—and he did go to confession (or at least he went into the confessional and stayed there a while before coming back out). And we did some more counseling together. One thing our therapist told us to do was to set up certain time blocks in which we would get together and discuss the state of our marriage. These were like "little dates"—without the romance. We would go somewhere to get some coffee, and that was the only time we could talk about marriage matters. The idea was to try to establish a life of normalcy and mutual trust, and not let the marriage/relationship discussion between us spill over into the rest of our lives. When we got home from our little coffee-filled dates, the home would remain neutral.

Back at the house, I had moved upstairs, and it was just me up there taking care of the dogs. That was my main living space, and I got to enjoy it. My domain—mine, all mine. For the first couple of months, he was gone probably five of those eight weekends, going back and forth to the East, maybe Florida, and a couple other places. I was keeping score at home. He had the master bedroom downstairs—trust me, I didn't want to be there—and I had a guest bedroom upstairs, which was already all furnished with a bed and, of course, a TV.

David would come home from work on a typical day and often he had had a lot to drink. I would go upstairs at that point, so that I didn't have to deal with him from seven o'clock at night on. Then in the morning, he was gone by the time I got up. At least that worked out well, timewise. Who knows what time he was passing out at night? I didn't have to care, nor did I bother. I had my own really comfy bed, my dogs, and a TV remote. Home sweet home.

By this time I had been prescribed what I needed to relax and to be able to sleep well: Ativan for anxiety and Ambien for the sleep itself. Ativan is similar to the better-known Xanax. The generic name for Ativan is lorazepam, which, according to webmd.com, is a medication that belongs to a class of drugs known as benzodiazepines. These produce a calming effect by acting on the brain and nerves that comprise our central nervous system. Ativan/lorazepam works by bolstering the effects of GABA, which is a naturally occurring chemical in our bodies.

You are probably more familiar with Ambien, also known generically as zolpidem. You guessed it: it's used to treat insomnia in adults. There was plenty of that going around in our house, for at least half of the human occupants. It helps you fall asleep faster, and from that alone it improved my quality of sleep. That isn't surprising when you consider that it is part of the drug class known as sedative/hypnotics. I don't know if I was ever actually "hypnotized" from taking it, but I had no complaints either. It still comes in handy from time to time. (You really didn't think that a busted marriage with a lowlife in conjunction with an adoption that failed to launch hits you only for a few months and then just fades away like magic, did you? It didn't for me. I wish you better luck if you are going through or have gone through what I did.)

As for drinking or eating in those next few months post-admission (a term I will use from now on to refer to David's one-foot-out-the-back-door confession that he had had extramarital sex, eventually to be disclosed as an affair), I was essentially doing little of either (drinking or eating). One of the only things I could stand to eat was Stouffer's mac and cheese, which has been described as "smooshy" and "mushy," meaning it tasted OK and slid down the throat into the stomach fairly easily. I needed that. I also knew I needed to be consuming something green—I did have to look out for my health after all, so I got lots of broccoli. That pretty much sums up all I ate for a long while, and I lost thirty-five pounds in six months. Nothing like finding out that your husband is having an affair during the adoption process to get you on track for getting down to your goal weight. Not that that was a high priority with me at the time.

I also did some jogging, or light running, just to work out and get fitter, both of body and mind, and it worked pretty well. To this day, I still jog a lot and it can help smooth out a lot of wrinkles (proverbially speaking) that otherwise can pretty much sink a day or a week for you. I couldn't eat anything until about three or four in the afternoon. Until then, I would just drink coffee and hang out on the phone talking with people while trying to figure things out. Chaos, while in limbo. Go figure. It was kind of weird, that time in limbo. I was overwhelmed, confused.

Dr. Doolittle

When he was at home at night, drunk, David would talk to Rudy, our dog, a West Highland white terrier, and he'd say things like, "Rudy, I'm going to get you your own lawyer." David was so inebriated that he didn't realize the decibel level at which he was talking. He was talking loud enough for me to hear him upstairs, even though I really wasn't making an effort to listen to any of this. Maybe you know how that goes when you are tuning someone out, or someone else on the phone is just down the hall around a corner from you, talking on the phone with someone:

you can hear a voice, but most of the time you aren't tuning in to pick up what actually is being said. I had no interest in eavesdropping on any of his conversations, even with a dog. But I did catch the part about his telling Rudy he might get him a lawyer—we hadn't even formally discussed the possibility of getting a divorce. Not yet at least. Although, thinking back, I sometimes pondered titling this book *Rudy's Lawyer: An Affair to Forget*. Or maybe subtitle it *The Journey Forward* instead.

As we began our attempt at reconciliation—and I, for one, was serious about giving it a go, asshole husband and all—we took a few trips, always a part of his job, me tagging along. There was Seattle. Martha's Vineyard. London. Then back to Seattle for a second go of it, and we certainly had a go of it there, and it wasn't good.

I was shocked when he asked me to join him in Seattle the first time around, at the beginning of June. It had been only four weeks since I had learned of his affair. Was he reaching out? He had gone to counseling with me and had been to church a couple of times, but he still wasn't being very forthcoming about things. More of nothing but bits and pieces about what had gone on between him and this other woman. He started talking some about it when we were having one of our coffee meetings, but he was definitely still guarded about the whole thing.

One thing noticeable about him was what I took to be newfound confidence. Plus he seemed alert and happy. But why the change? Of course I was suspicious that there was something else still going on, but if there was, he wasn't going there. He was no longer having to hide it, but he was still lying. Some lying, some not telling the whole truth when he was recounting aspects of his relationship—a little bit of this, a little bit of that. I tried to ask him questions, but there were no answers there. One thing it took me a while to realize was, that at no point, at least in the early going, did he say that the affair was over.

Plus, I was having trouble with the boundaries at home—I couldn't handle having just that two-hour block of time at the coffee shop once or twice a week. I needed information, not lies, not deflections, no BS whatsoever. It had now been a month, and I still didn't really know what was up with them. But that 2:00-4:00 time frame is what the therapist Melanie had given us. It was on the weekends only and at that coffee shop we had picked out. We got some things accomplished, but it was always the same muckety-muck—once we got started and began warming up (not to be confused with warming up to each other in an emotional or, God forbid, a sexual sense). We would start breaking ground and getting somewhere . . . then our time would be up, and that was it for him. He was done. Toast. Each and every time, pretty much. There was more I wanted and needed to know. Sometimes I would have these sobbing moments, and Melanie had told me that he shouldn't pander to me in those times, so I just had to plow my way through them somehow. He needed to let me process through those things. At times it worked, at others, not so much.

The book Melanie gave us to read (I actually did read it, as she instructed) is *Getting Past the Affair,* by Douglas K. Snyder, Donald H. Baucom, and Kristina Coop

Gordon. They go at the subject from a variety of different angles, covering everything from whether the marriage itself is to blame to asking the question of how my partner could have done this. One of many things that jumped out at me in reading—and at times studying— the book was the question, "Were we ever a healthy couple?" The easy answer when you've been through the lingering hell of having a partner who cheated on you is "Hell, yes," but in many cases that fails to account for everything that came before and which you have tossed into a trunk that is locked and stowed away in the back of your brain (the ultimate compartmentalization), marked "Not to be opened until the Year 2045." I believe David and I did have a healthy marriage in the beginning and for at least seven years, and Snyder, Baucom, and Gordon offer up an interesting perspective in that regard:

> In the initial chaos following an affair, it's sometimes possible to lose a broader view of the marriage from a long-term perspective. As an injured partner, it may be difficult to recall earlier times when you were confident in the love and commitment you each brought to your marriage because right now you feel deeply hurt. Or you may now view those earlier confident feelings with suspicion, perhaps doubting your judgment or questioning how truthful your partner has ever been with you. As a participating partner, it may be difficult to focus on what you've valued most in your marriage because this seems at such odds with your decision to have an affair. "How could I have done this but still believe our getting married was the right decision?"

In evaluating whether you can make this marriage work again—and whether you even want to—you need to consider not only what was happening in the few months leading up to the affair, but also the broader picture of your marriage from the very beginning. What were the good reasons for marrying your partner? What have been your most worthwhile times together? It may also be true that there have been some important vulnerabilities in your marriage from the outset.[1]

Later, the authors make a point well worth remembering in terms of perspective and tolerating the bad with the good. It doesn't do much good for me in regard to my former marriage and subsequent divorce (after all, it ended more than ten years ago), but it's something every married couple should have hammered into their heads before they walk down the aisle:

> *No partner is perfect.* Successful marriages are those in which the partners grow together despite their short-comings, care for each other despite their flaws and dif-ferences, and nurture their respective strengths in order to hold on to the good and minimize the bad in their relationship. What were the good qualities that drew you to each other? Were there fundamental flaws in your relationship or in each other that you overlooked? Can you recover the best parts of your relationship and each other that, at one time, made you want to spend the rest of your lives together?"[2]

Getting back to the session with Melanie, the bit about having to plow ahead in processing the affair and its effects on *me*, left me too afraid to move forward in any direction in my life. My choices were either to move back to the New Jersey area, return to Memphis, or stay in California. Let's think about that. I had grown up in New Jersey and still had plenty of friends based there—plus my father's side of the family was still living there, and I knew that they loved me. And it had been over a year since I had moved from there. I just wasn't processing—not a whole lot of that in California. Or I could go back to Memphis and be with, or at least near, my mom and sister. Or I could just stay on the West Coast. None of the options had a lot of appeal to me; all three of them were plain scary.

That brings me back to what the therapist had said about Rachel A and Rachel B. The questions I was asking were about how do *we* move forward rather than focusing on what had just happened. What's the next development in our relationship?

Blowup

It was during our second trip to Seattle that summer—this time in August—that things went haywire. I was about to type in " . . . things went a *little* haywire . . . " but no sense in softening what really happened. By this time, we were three months into our attempt at a reconciliation. While we weren't digging in as deeply as I thought we should be on aspects of his affair, we were having some good moments. Not a lot of intimacy, but we did have a few laughs and moments about as close to tender as you could get without being awkward and regretful.

All things considered, summer up until Seattle Part II was just a lot of back and forth. One step forward, one step back. This second Seattle trip was for him to attend a conference at which he was going to be speaking to a group, and it was a big deal for him. It's understandable. Whether small audience or large, public speaking is still public speaking, and that has long been regarded as one of man's (and woman's) greatest fears.

I'm sure Zig Ziglar was still getting butterflies late in his motivational speaking career, and I'm guessing that the likes of Tony Robbins still get some clammy hands each time they get up in front of a crowd. I can relate at some level—teachers do a lot of standup five days a week, thirty-six-plus weeks a year, and I don't mean comedy. Not intentional anyway.

Seattle was a dividing point in our Marriage Part II. It was the next significant event to come my way—I would say *our* way, except he instigated it; I was there only to feel the brunt of the tsunami. In basketball terms, it's called taking a charge on defense. Here we were in Seattle, and David and his (still!) mistress were about to knock me to the deck with a tag-team charge of their own.

On the day that David was giving his presentation—he was scheduled to speak fairly early in the morning (at least early by my clock)—we had kissed goodbye. We were going to meet up later on. After waking up, I got out of bed and started walking toward the bathroom, when I spotted a little white piece of paper lying in the middle of the floor. I picked it up and saw that there was a telephone number written on it. *That's strange,* I thought. We had been living on the West Coast for however long, and I could see that it was a New Jersey area code.

The wheels started turning, and I quickly felt flushed in the face, and my heartbeat quickened. Even though I had still been dealing with an ever-present sense of anxiety and distrust, this was a jolt that I hadn't felt in a while. It had been about three months now. I grabbed my phone and called the number, and it was a florist in the New Jersey area, near where we had once lived. I hung up; I needed to think this through, figure out how to proceed. I needed answers.

I waited five or ten minutes, then called back, knowing what I was going to say. When someone at the florist shop answered, I said, "This is David Franken's administrative assistant and I'm trying to reconcile his books. Can you tell me what he recently ordered from your shop?"

And the woman on the other end said, "No, ma'am, I can't do that. We have a policy of not discussing orders with anyone but the client himself or herself."

"OK, I understand," I said to her. "But please do this for me. I just need the number—the amount—that was paid, that's all I need."

I was doing my best just to make it sound like this was routine for me, that he depended on me to reconcile the books, and he was always missing the mark on turning in his receipts. She put me on hold for about three or four minutes. Then she came back and said, "Yeah, it was seventy-five dollars to Avery Martini for a Happy Birthday arrangement."

"Great, thank you very much," I said before I hung up. Busted! Again.

I sit here and ponder this great mystery of the universe, how my husband, the beloved David, ever got himself into this mess in the first place. Exactly how does one spouse turn his or her back on an ordained marriage and not only become infatuated with someone else outside the marriage, but end up screwing them for who knows how long, then lying about it the whole time during an adoption process? Again, I turn to authors Snyder, Baucom, and Gordon for some answers, and here's a small chunk of what they offer regarding how one partner even got involved in the first place:

> Before you, the injured partner, try to answer this question, we first want to provide you with a way of thinking about factors that might have contributed to your partner's vulnerability to an affair. Some of these may extend well back in time and involve attitudes, beliefs, anxieties, needs, or other tendencies that were in place before you and your partner ever met. Examples might include unrealistic beliefs about how a marriage is supposed to be, lack of confidence in oneself as an intimate partner, or an inability to withstand long periods of unhappiness or stress without much support or relief. Think of such factors as paving the way for an affair. They don't cause an affair to happen, but they can raise the vulnerability or risk of an affair if certain other conditions come along.

Other factors that made the affair more likely to occur may have predated it by only weeks or months, such as flirting with someone who was also susceptible to an affair, developing an emotionally intimate relationship and spending increasing time alone with someone else, or seeking the company of the opposite sex when traveling out of town on business. Such behaviors don't inevitably lead to an affair, but they clearly lower the safeguards and raise the risks.[3]

A shower and makeup could wait. I threw on a skirt and top, marched to the elevator, punched the button for the floor where the conference room was located, and proceeded to the room in which he was speaking. I opened the door, stepped inside, and from the back of the room made it clear, after catching his eye with a couple of hand signals, that I needed him to come back there so I could speak to him *now*. No way this was going to wait until coffee between 2:00 and 4:00 P.M. What better time to stray outside that boundary? I considered walking right up to the front of the room and grabbing him by the ear or his tie and yanking him out of the room. He quickly spotted me and gave me one of those looks that said, "Wait a minute; I'll be with you as soon as I can."

Another ten minutes or so went by before he finished and came through the door to join me out in the hallway, where I was seething, with steam coming out of my ears and nostrils. Once he came out to see me, we found the nearest door to the outside and started walking on the boardwalk leading toward Puget Sound. As we walked away, I told him, "This is what I just found," and I shoved the piece of paper in his face. His look of shock and resignation, accompanied by a drawn-out "Ahhhhhhhh," told me that he knew immediately he had once again messed up.

Sometime later, after I had calmed down, it occurred to me that maybe he had purposely dropped the piece of paper there knowing I would find it, as if he wanted me to know this was going on. I've read those stories about how a crook will actually leave behind clues hoping he (or she) will get caught, almost like a cry for help for whatever it is that is driving them to do whatever it is they aren't supposed to be doing. Then again, it might have just fallen out of his pants pocket.

By now, with us outside of the hotel, I was screaming at him. *"How could you do this? We were going to reconcile! We've been to counseling. We've been to church. We've done the things we need to be doing. How could you do this?!"*

"It was the final nail in the coffin," David said. "This was me saying goodbye to her."

"Sending flowers is not a goodbye. But good try," I countered.

It wasn't long before a security guard came. My yelling at David had caught his attention. David wasn't getting loud, though. What could he get mad about? He was caught red-handed, with his pants down! He was at a loss for words, just taking his whipping. I said, "I have more to do here." I made him call her, right there from the boardwalk, as I stood there with him, ready to get to the bottom of this. I was now reaching out to grab my share of control of the situation.

He called her a couple of times, but she wasn't answering. I said, "Call again. And this time leave a message." This time when he called, he stayed on the line as her outgoing greeting played through. Then he said, "It's over. Rachel found out that I sent you flowers, and I'm really sorry about all this." He said a few other meaningless words, and then he hung up.

"How do I know if you just really left a message? Call back again," I told David.

This time she picked up, and he said, "We have to end it."

I knew she was on the phone because I put my ear up to it and could hear her speaking. David basically said to her that he was sorry, that I had found out about the flowers he sent her, and just a lot of other blah, blah, blah. After their short chat, he handed me the phone and said, "Thank you. You saved me."

Before I continue with this remarkable story of in-your-face (and on-the-phone) adultery, to this day I still ask myself, *Why did this creep continue with the affair even after I had confronted him and found out about it, and he had committed (at least verbally) to working toward a reconciliation with me?* In addressing this conundrum, Snyder et al, in *Getting Past the Affair,* uncannily describe a scenario that sounds like they could have been spying on David and Avery. (I mean, we're talking unhinged knuckleheads here, aren't we?)

A brief affair ended by the participating partner creates its own trauma. But when a partner continues involvement in an affair, maintaining the illicit relationship usually requires repeated lies that compound the trauma further. Elaborate cover stories are constructed to conceal secret trysts. Telephone bills for the cell phone used to call the other person may be sent to work or to an undisclosed post office box; separate e-mail accounts and texts under the guise of a company for which he had worked, used solely for exchanges with the outside person are kept secret. Gifts for the other person are purchased in cash or with a separate credit card known only to the participating partner. Perhaps most painful of all, the participating partner may continue to be emotionally or sexually intimate with his spouse as though the outside relationship doesn't even exist. This ability to separate the outside relationship from interactions with the injured partner so completely may seem incomprehensible.[4]

Sadly, this was us.

The authors then list five possible reasons that the cheating spouse feels emboldened to continue in the affair beyond what any reasonable person would likely describe as a "brief affair":

- "Emotional attachment or feelings of responsibility to the outside person."
- "Positive aspects of the outside relationship."
- "Pessimism about the outcome of the marriage."
- "Feelings of entitlement or lack of concern about 'getting caught.'"

99

- "Mentally separating and isolating the marriage and outside relationship."[5]

The whole thing at the Seattle hotel was horrible. I went back to our hotel room and started calling her myself. I must have called her twenty times. I already had her number; now I knew exactly where she was—home. She finally picked up on about the twentieth time I called. I had a whole bunch of questions that I asked her and I learned a lot, as she stayed on the phone with me. It was another thirty minutes or so before David got back to the room, so I was able to have plenty of quality time with her.

We did a lot of talking, and almost all of it was initiated by questions that I asked her. Again, I refer to my journal, another segment of which follows, with some minor editing for clarification:

- I learned that they took a trip to Florida in October or November (the year before) with me in California in the apartment.
- He's met her parents and brother, and been to her home several times.
- He's told her he loves her several times.
- She slept in our marital bed fewer than six times.
- She never saw his new wedding ring in March. (I bought him a new wedding ring because he apparently lost his old one.)
- In May I asked him to come clean. (But) he sees her and has her spend the night at the Hilton.
- (According to her) David said, "I told her I was unhappy and that it was (my) choice to go to the West

Coast." He told her that we were not physical, which was a lie.

- She said she felt loved by him.
- (Writing about me) Being an emotional mess has turned into anger. All seems clear to me.
- I also learned that she called, and they spoke on his birthday. Then, only last weekend, he called her from the Minnesota cabin.

We also discussed how he was cheap, dishonest, and narcissistic. He took advantage of our respective trust for him. She also said that he's a coward.

We were pretty well into the conversation when I finally got around to telling her that I was having trouble with the duration of their relationship, how long it had been going on. It was a pretty long phone call. After David got back to the room, he sat on the bed and listened to me as I continued to talk to her and ask her questions.

I was thankful for that little white piece of paper with the telephone number, because it catapulted me into action. It woke me back up to what had been going on and was still going on, even three months post-admission.

I drank a whole bottle of wine on the flight home. We had one first-class ticket and one coach for the trip back—and you'd better believe it, I sat in first class. I sat next to a friend who also worked at David's company, and, once home, she helped me find a good lawyer. In fact, a lot of people from his company were on that flight. Did I mention that I drank a lot on the way home? You bet.

The very next day, back at home unsweet home, as soon as I got up out of bed, I called the movers—the same movers that about a year earlier had moved us cross country to California. The movers came out a few days later—no, I hadn't packed in that short a time—so I could start the process of getting estimates for my move back to Tennessee. I was still living upstairs at the house, taking care of myself, and going to therapy, except this time everyone knew that I would soon be leaving. It was still August, and I knew I wouldn't be working at a school because I hadn't been out west long enough to get a full-time faculty job there. In the meantime I had been running a tutoring business—math and reading—and had a couple of kids with whom I was working.

About a week after that second Seattle trip, and a few days after the preliminary meeting with the movers, I flew back out to Memphis to stay with Corinne and get some more much-needed mental and emotional well-being rehab. Plus, of course, I needed to start looking for a place to live once I moved back there. However much time I could spend at my sister's, it was going to be short term. That was only fair to her. Here's what I wrote in my journal on my first night at Corinne's:

> Up all night tormented with images and thoughts and the fact that there could be more hurtful information. Feeling so hurt about the levels to which he took the affair. Feeling anxious and worried about how this divorce will all work out. I cannot live with the choices he has made. He has taken advantage of me and our relationship. He has humiliated me. He has said he misses me and wants this to work. I hope he understands that I cannot go forward with him and that he is making this easier on my heart, which

I'll figure out later on.

We will have to be mindful of each other during this very difficult time. I think it will be very difficult once we together decide that this is going to happen and he travels, et cetera.

These are my observations about David:

- I feel more alone with him than when I'm alone.
- He acts indifferent and cold toward me.
- He hasn't consistently gone to therapy or church.
- I will always be and feel lied to with him.
- Will always worry about his phone and his travel.
- I will always be second, third, or an afterthought, with his work coming first.
- I must remember that it's an old, lonely, cold relationship.
- He does not nurture me.
- He cuts me off when I'm speaking.
- Most likely I will always feel angry, confused, anxious, and wonder if I made the right choice staying with him.
- The trust and respect for him is gone.
- He will always be narcissistic and dominant.
- A leopard doesn't change its spots.
- Unilaterally, he made a decision that we will not adopt.
- Does not consider what I am going through regarding the affair.
- Sent her flowers. P.S. He bought me flowers after the Seattle debacle . . . I threw them at him, then he cleaned them up.
- Called her back after we decided to move forward.

- He is an untrained dog who pisses on everything.
- After arguments going forward together, I will be resentful and regretful that I gave it another try.
- Continued lies about phone call on his fiftieth birthday and his call from the cabin to her.
- He will always flirt and look at other women.
- I must remember that when I pulled back from our relationship, I saw very little effort on his part to nurture or keep our marriage going, which is very important.
- Remember how indifferent and cold he was when he told me he didn't want to adopt.
- Booked flight to London with her while his brother was visiting us, and two weeks later tells me while his mother is visiting he doesn't want to adopt.
- He makes me feel like a doormat, lied to constantly, and he's totally insensitive.
- He steals my light.
- I fear a serious loss of self with him.
- He is a liar about everything.

It was while I was at my sister's house in Memphis that same week that it hit me: I had lost my best friend, even though he really hadn't been my friend in a long time. He no longer was listening to me and had been treating me with indifference for a very long time; not just months, but years, and especially since May. He had never even asked me what I needed, even as just a courtesy. Even though he had not done anything extra-special nice for me post-admission—and you would have thought he'd at least try to do something as part of a purposeful reconciliation attempt—I realized that not all men are like this. I never got to the point where I became so discouraged that I was ready to write off all men just because of the skunk that he was.

On my last full day at Corinne's in Memphis, I started to feel very nervous about going back to California the next day and having to deal with him up close. He texted me a bunch of times that day asking for forgiveness, but that was just him going through the motions. I knew I could no longer live that life with him, knowing what he had done to me and our marriage. Yeah, I had a sense of dread of having to be back at our house with him in it, but I sure was excited about getting to see Rudy and Cooper, the dogs, once again. That thought cheered me up some.

7

The Divorce

Bᴀᴄᴋ ʜᴏᴍᴇ ɪɴ ᴄᴀʟɪғᴏʀɴɪᴀ, ɪᴛ ᴛᴏᴏᴋ ᴛᴡᴏ ᴏʀ ᴛʜʀᴇᴇ ᴡᴇᴇᴋs ғᴏʀ ᴜs ᴛᴏ ᴅɪᴠᴠʏ ᴜᴘ ᴏᴜʀ ʙᴇʟᴏɴɢɪɴɢs ᴀɴᴅ ᴘᴏs-sᴇssɪᴏɴs. Everything that was mine was packed up and stacked in the garage. By now it was September, although I didn't leave until November, meaning I was still living there for another two uncomfortable months.

I was still just trying to figure everything out with where things were headed, but David couldn't help with anything. He just couldn't; he wasn't capable of it. Our relationship, or what was left of it, wasn't high up on his list of priorities. His work was number one—just like always.

I was gathering up my belongings, getting packed, and storing things in the garage. I think he really wanted me to stay—at least he wanted me to believe that, yes, he had a girlfriend, but that I just needed to let it go and move forward. But that was something I just could not process. He wanted me to think that his affair was over—there was no longer a relationship there—but I knew he wasn't over her, and apparently she was still in the game, with him.

Going back to that time we had been to Seattle on that business trip, where I had found the white slip of paper with the florist's phone number on it, I'm sure he called her back soon after I had forced him to make that call to her in my presence. No doubt, in his following up with her, he had assured her that he had made that call only because I was standing right there, and that the truth was that he still wanted to be with her and keep the relationship going.

The frustration of talking with David makes me sure of my decision, which was to move out and back to Memphis and to file for divorce. He was cold and distant, and he didn't try to understand me. For starters, he could have started asking me questions to get to know me better—finally. Uh-uh; none of that. Nothing had changed. He wasn't willing to discuss what he had done. Plus, he was having trouble with involving our therapist. He had neither shown remorse nor given a true indication that he wanted our marriage to continue.

David said he was embarrassed and ashamed to discuss the affair. All he would say was that he would contact our therapist when he had the time. Then he proceeded to list all the things that made him busy, such as his involvement at work with acquisitions, and so on and so forth. Blah, blah, blah. One thing he did say, offering a glimmer of consideration for me, was that he had ordered the UBS paperwork I had asked to see detailing all of our finances. That was just one more area in which I had been kept in the dark. Now, though, I was coming out of my shell.

I hadn't brought up the issue of divorce yet, though. Even when we were divvying up the possessions and everything else, I think he thought I would just stash everything in the garage indefinitely, and that the biggest leap I would eventually make would be some sort of separation, with this idea—presumably his—that we would eventually get back together and things would somehow work themselves out. I knew that wasn't the likely course of action, but I was not ready to talk about divorce yet. Or at least to formalize the process.

Still, he couldn't handle my feelings. He would walk away, fidget with paperwork, or glance at the TV (it was turned on). He asked, "What do you want me to do?" I said, "I have given you a list of things, and it's not my job to tell you what to do—what extra-special things to do." Face it, he had skewed ideas, such as sending her flowers as a goodbye. What a joke. The kind that elicits no laughter, at least not from me.

There was always the frustration of trying to talk with David, which only made me feel so much more sure about my decision to divorce him. Following is a slightly edited version of a segment from my journal at the time, dated August 30 and 31, not long after we had returned from that trip to Seattle:

August 30:

He is not willing to make the effort necessary for this marriage to continue. Tonight's conversation makes me really want to let him have it good.

He has skewed ideas, such as he didn't leave it open-ended all summer (with his girlfriend), but she feels he did.

August 31:

Many people can wipe the slate clean, but there must be effort and remorse on the unfaithful person's part. He says he can't live like this, that I'm pushing him away and that he can't get a word in.

He has clearly fallen into old patterns of working too long and hard. He is running and burying just like when he worked in New York. I thought he learned from that.

I told him he doesn't care about me. He says he does. But he doesn't care about me in the way I need. He says he works because he's married. Otherwise, he has enough money and would live a simple life. How foolish. David is not much without his power and position. He would be stupid to quit, couldn't afford his home, especially with only half of what he would be left with.

I called his girlfriend again at one point after we had gotten back from Seattle. I was still trying to find out more about what had gone on between them, and this was while we were still redoing the house. The floor was being ripped out and the walls were being painted, and she was asking, "What's all that noise?" She could hear it all over the phone, going on in the background. I could tell it shocked her when I told her we were redoing the house, the fact that we were still investing in it.

On that same day, I called her again because I needed to find out more about him and what he was like around her. Following are some of the highlights from that conversation, which I revisit here just to give some added perspective on how he was perceived by someone else who loved him. Going back over this helps reinforce for me why I needed to get out of this marriage and get on with life without him, for good:

- Her previous relationship ended badly, so she's even more hurt by this because he knew that.
- He told her he had never done this before.
- She slept in our guest bedroom and master bedroom and parked in our garage two or three times when I was visiting my mother, who was having chemo treatments.
- She feels naïve and foolish. He washed the sheets after one of my trips to be with Mom. Really!
- He asked a lot of questions about her former husband, like "How did you know when it was over?"
- David once gave me a company shirt, and when I didn't want it, he gave it to her.
- She wondered why he told me.
- The two most hurtful parts to hear about during this conversation were the parts about her sleeping in our home and telling her that he loved her within days after my confronting him about the affair.

It's also worth mentioning that I would eventually find out that one of his friends who was also a friend of mine had been in on this, knowing the whole time what was going on and helping to cover for David. That hurt.

Separate and Unequal

Here it was September, and by now I knew that I would be separating from David—moving out—in November. My mom was going to fly out to California to help me finish packing and then join me for the drive back to Tennessee. She, of course, would also help me with the driving; it was a long haul, more than two thousand miles. My mom never really liked him, and neither did my sister. Especially Corinne. Everything had been set in motion for us to leave in the next day or two. All this was becoming real to me: David had his girlfriend, like it or not; I was about to leave him, for good; and we were eventually going to be divorced, sooner or later.

The movers were coming early in the morning, a day or two after that glorious night with the three of us eating out. The truck arrived, and as soon as it got loaded with all my stuff, it was time for Mom and me to leave. David was milling around while this was going on, and as Mom and I got into the car, he asked me not to do this—really, what the hell was he thinking?—"You don't have to do this," but then nothing. He didn't even try to offer a lame rationalization for why I should stay. I think we briefly hugged before I got into the car with my mom to drive away.

Even though everything had been in motion for us to leave, it was still hard. I left that house behind feeling numb. I was a mess for a long time and wasn't thinking clearly. I was sad and quiet, confused. A part of me thought he might follow me to Tennessee so he could catch up with me and say, "Let's work this out," but that never happened. In fact, I had that same thought play over and over in my head for the first few months that I was on my own, for real. But then I got a great job, in a school of course, and things started to come together for me pretty well.

Pay Attention: Here's the Juice

Okay, let's talk about the divorce. The juicy stuff, right? Well, maybe not so much. It wasn't that complicated: he had an affair (that was still going full speed ahead, it seems) and we didn't have any children. I got some furniture and other belongings I wanted to take with me back to Tennessee; he would get to keep the rest. I had been a good girl—no affairs, no blowing his brains out—and I was going to get some money from him for a while. He was going to get to keep most of what he had, and we could just move away from each other, in every way conceivable. I still had my joint Visa card, and he was responsible for paying it off, even though the divorce got a bit more expensive than it needed to be. And that's what many attorneys do—run up their bills—and divorce lawyers certainly are not an exception to that rule.

I filed for divorce a month or two before I left California to drive back to Tennessee, which puts that in

September or October of that year. I didn't have any money in hand, so I grabbed our joint Visa card and took out a $20,000 advance on it. I immediately gave it over to my attorney for his retainer to draw against as he worked through our divorce case. I had actually been through two attorneys before I shelled out the twenty big ones to Attorney No. 3. One was for mediation that didn't work out, and then the second one I didn't like; no explanation needed. This one guy, the third guy, Billy Austin, was someone that my friend Liesl had recommended to me. He was really expensive, but he was supposed to be the best divorce lawyer in northern California, and I liked him a lot as soon as I met him.

Let me retrace my steps some and talk about why the idea of mediation didn't work out for us. At first I was willing to go into mediation with David because I thought that's what would have been better for us. If he were for it, it would be easier for us to settle. At least that was my reasoning. Plus it's a lot less expensive than plowing through a full divorce, where the meter is almost always running, and for months, even years, on end. There were no kids involved, and it seemed like mediation was the way to go. The problem was that there would be no one representing my best interests. I hadn't thought that through very well in my initial willingness to go the mediation route, but then the reality of what was at stake hit me. Mediation would be just one person for the both of us, and I knew I needed to have someone in the room that would be in there for me. Otherwise, it's just a roll of the dice. Besides, I had become extremely leery of anything he suggested. He would probably finagle things in his favor by getting someone who claimed to be a mediator but was in truth a friend of his. I didn't know what he was up to, but I also know the days of my trusting him had gone by the wayside.

Which brings me back to the issue of money. Billy's upfront retainer fee was $25,000. I told him that I didn't have that, but I could give him $20,000. He balked some at first, but he settled for that as his starting fee. After consulting with him and answering his questions about our marriage, the problems, the ditched adoption, and the ongoing affair, Billy told me that he would draw up the papers and get them ready to be served to David. Hot damn, that ball was rolling downhill now.

That was a fun day, filing for the divorce. Taking the money off the credit card knowing I wasn't going to have to pay any of it back was pure bliss; I actually felt a chill go up my spine. While I was in Billy's office getting things started, I went through all the initial questions and paperwork with him. That's all that had to be done at that point—nothing in terms of discovery or interrogatories before I left for Memphis.

When I left Billy's office, I felt nervous, but it was a good nervous. It was closer to giddiness, like I was jumping up and down and clicking my heels in my head, over and over. I quickly called Corinne and Mom and told them that I had done it, that I had filed for divorce; it was like I was in a movie. I had the chills and was shaking with joy, like I was in the middle of opening the best Christmas present ever. This must be what it feels like exiting a bad marriage with a dirty scoundrel—I felt a palpable sense of freedom, even though I knew there were still hoops to jump through before the divorce would become official. I turned up the music so loud as I ran errands.

I did a lot of driving around that day and ended the day by going to David's office to tell him I had filed for divorce and he would soon be served, although, obviously, I didn't have those papers with me. That would take another few days for Billy to pull that together and then get a professional server to carry out the delivery mission.

When I broke the news to David, he said, "I sort of thought that would be happening, but all I ask is that you don't have me served here at work." So I had him served at the house, and then it was time for me to vamoose so he could sit there and enjoy looking through the papers on his own, without me around him to ruin the moment for him. He had earned this moment for himself; now it would be his turn to enjoy the spoils.

But this thing was far from over.

Learning about Me

Let me again pause from the narrative to go back over a journal entry I made around the time I filed, on October 1, in fact, and which was especially meaningful to me. I was still more than a month away from moving back to Memphis, but this is important because after months of carrying around that PTSD of mine and going through counseling, I was beginning to learn more about myself, and that alone was putting me on more solid ground. Here are some more of my journal excerpts, which I had written down:

October 1:

The first day of a new month, the first day of moving forward in a new direction and feeling strong. Although it's a damp, gloomy, cold day in California, I have been given the opportunity to read in bed and write in my new journal. Also, I have been given the gift of being able to see that this is the first day in a new month where my future and feelings are on a more solid ground than they have been in five months.

Okay. And then this page is what I have learned about me.

I am a verbal processor. I am too tolerant, allow myself to be steamrolled. I don't face things. I take the easy way out and reorganize to make things work for me. I become complacent and defer far too easily and quickly. I cannot allow him the peace of mind of putting his head in the sand about what he's done. Need to do better, follow up.

I don't have a well-developed guard or warrior within me. I need to put my worth out there. I tell myself half-truths. I am courageous and strong. I overperformed where David underperformed.

I do not feel seen or heard by most people. I have strong endurance. I need to help me see the big picture, to become more social and quick, and to develop more protection or a more guarded warrior. (I talk about this more in the next chapter, referring to a book I was told to read in the early going of my counseling sessions.)

I do not have any real married role models to see what is healthy.

I am grateful for my family, having choices and options, beautiful days, healthy family, my education, my own health, good friends, Cooper and Rudy, supportive family and friends, a place to go, a new home, a new job, a better relationship with God.

What I like to do: Go to bed with a good magazine; walk and play with Cooper and Rudy; cook a good meal with good wine; drink good coffee; nap; send out small gifts, cards too; make healthy juice; run; be outside; get up early.

These are the things I'm looking forward to: Watching B (my nephew/Corinne's son) grow up; spending time with B; being close to Corinne, her husband, B, and Mom; the holidays; craft fairs; being independent; the cabin; teaching; a new home; Cooper and Rudy; Shelby Farms; peaceful life; discovering myself; meeting someone someday; buying an airline ticket; booking a trip or cruise on my own; a new baby for my sister.

Here's the stunner about the divorce: it took two years for it to be finalized. And get this, we never saw the inside of a courtroom. That deserves an explanation and here it is: in a nutshell, it's two attorneys—one representing each side of the case—dragging things out with a whole lot of this and a whole lot of that, dozens of ticky-tacky things flying back and forth in a marathon game of give and take, like a championship chess match between two masters—each one makes a move, he or she hits the timer so the opponent's clock starts—and all this costing hundreds of dollars an hour. David dragged his feet. By the time this nutty game was done, so much of it seemed such a waste. I used my alimony to pay for every dime.

Part of the deal, too, was that David was consistently in and out of the country during those two years, as part of his job, gumming up the legal process in the meantime. I also had a ton of stuff I needed to do myself. I had told him he needed to get a lawyer and he said, "No, I'm going to be on my own." Eventually, he did get his own lawyer but he kept saying, "People like us, we don't have to spend a lot of money on lawyers."

Speak for yourself, pal. I said, "I do—I need my interests properly represented and in the best way." From there, it just worked out, David's lawyer working things out with my lawyer over the phone, trying to settle things equitably.

One key point about the marital dissolution agreement (MDA): I hadn't wanted to put anything in there about marital misconduct on David's part, although it had occurred in a big way and had already been admitted and proven. I just put in irreconcilable differences, which is pretty much standard wording for an MDA. My intent in leaving out the part about marital misconduct wasn't to give David a break; no way in hell. I just knew if I had put it in there, it would have ruffled his feathers enough for him to go into his typical manipulation mode, inserting lies and rationalizations into the process that would only have complicated things, bumped up the attorney's fees even more, and led to who knows what else. I don't regret it, not one bit. Everybody involved knew what had happened, and it wouldn't have any bearing on our situation one way or another. I wrote dozens of short, classy notes to wedding guests who had attended our wedding. They read something like this: "David has betrayed me. After therapy and dropping thirty-five pounds, I'm headed back to Tennessee." David did not like this *one bit*!

It was a ridiculous two-year process. It was a lot of my waiting for him to pay me money that he had been ordered to pay me on a monthly basis during the divorce process, what usually is a temporary deal leading up to the judge's divorce decree, even though we never actually saw a judge, either. Everything done for the divorce happened over the phone, with the occasional email or piece of postal mail. For a while I thought I might have to go back to California during the process, but that never happened, which was A-OK with me. David sometimes mentioned meeting in Denver to talk things through, but each time he brought it up, I said no. I told him to let the attorneys hammer it out. That's why we are already paying them.

There was a lot of back and forth, and David kept putting the brakes on. Billy kept me abreast of everything that was going on. I still had to pay him every month, in addition to the upfront payment. I don't know what David paid for his legal representation. It just dragged on for too long; the attorneys should have gotten the divorce done sooner.

Divorcing for Dollars

I don't have a lot of advice to pass along here in terms of how to manage a divorce, because there's not a whole lot either of the spouse's parties can do once the process has been turned over to their respective legal representatives. Every little thing that an attorney does on your behalf, whether it be to draw up an MDA, have a fifteen-minute phone call with you, or have one of their assistants or clerks type up a letter for you, or put something in the mail to you, you are being charged by the hour. The meter is always running.

If I had a do-over, at the start I would tell my attorney this needs to be done by a certain date—whatever it takes and whatever concessions need to be made, as long as both parties are feeling the effects of any compromise and you don't get taken advantage of. There was no reason for our divorce to be dragged out as it had—although I realize I can only say that now in hindsight, more than ten years after the fact. There were a lot of things that had to be fixed in the MDA as well as other things that had to be tweaked here and there. Ka-ching! Over and over, and over again. It was all financial stuff that had to be fixed— what could be moved, what couldn't be moved, and how much; and what would go to me and what he would get to keep. Garbage in, garbage out. It was all explained to me as we went along, as much as I could understand each time. The moral of the story is to get it done quickly so both of you can move on that much quicker.

I can't give you a step-by-step primer on what to expect and how to handle each step along the way. Even if I had a law degree and experience handling divorces, each case is different. The intents and expectations of each spouse give rise to any number of variables that can distinguish one divorce case from another.

I will share with you some general thoughts about preparing for and getting a divorce, which I gleaned from the Snyder, Baucom, and Gordon book, *Getting Past the Affair*:

> The list of items to consider when pursuing separation or divorce is potentially endless, but broad themes include pragmatic concerns related to living arrangements, finances, division of property, and informing others. . . .
>
> If possible, it's important for you and your partner to discuss where each of you will live in the short term during the separation process and in the longer term once the separation or divorce is complete. Some couples manage to stay in the same house through part or most of the initial process, working together to sort through financial issues or prepare their home for sale. More often, one partner finds a place to live temporarily until more permanent arrangements can be made. If separating, determine who will be responsible for which bills until the divorce is finalized—including house or car payments, credit card debts, clothing or medical expenses for the children, and so on. You may need to evaluate your own work situation and ensure that you will have adequate income once your relationship ends. Initial discussions about shared property may be useful, particularly as these relate to major purchases you might face when setting up separate households. You may also need to discuss how to divide assets that have special emotional meaning or how to divide or share pets. Avoid

arguing over 'pots and pans'—relatively small items of little emotional value that can easily be replaced.[1]

Actions speak louder than words, even in the legal arena. When it comes to the divorce process, move quickly—as much as you can.

8

The Wild Woman

DON'T GET THE WRONG IDEA: I'm not advising women who have just gone through a divorce to shed the boundaries and get a second wind sowing her wild oats, now that she's again a free agent. Not to mention that, by now, she is probably in her thirties, forties, or older, when being a wild child just isn't a good look.

When I speak of "the wild woman," I am talking about serious self-examination of where you have been, who you are, and what you really want to be, and what comprises the female psyche. Through counseling and reading a book my therapist assigned to me, I discovered how women have an instinctual nature consisting of two or more beings clashing inside of her. Oftentimes it is the submissive side—you might even call it the naïve side— that is allowed to win out in this inner struggle. At such times, women fall prey to the lustful Bluebeards of the world, whose aim in this dance of the genders is to control and dehumanize women. I experienced some of that in my marriage, but I wasn't equipped well enough then to recognize it. Nor did I have it in me to reach for and utilize my superpower to prevent it from controlling me. I don't see myself as a victim in my marriage; more like a willing participant, with David being permitted to call all the shots. As a totally submissive wife, I allowed myself to be victimized.

The book my therapist gave me to read is *Women Who Run with the Wolves: Myths and Stories of the Wild Woman Archetype*, a *New York Times* bestseller authored by Clarissa Pinkola Estés, PhD. I never met Dr. Estés—never had reason or occasion to, but according to her bio in the book (my edition was published in 1995), Dr. Estés at the time was a senior Jungian psychoanalyst who had been teaching and practicing for twenty-five years. She was also described as a cantadora, a "keeper of the old stories in the Latina tradition." That sounds mysterious, like she was some sort of wizened sage from another world or dimension. But I can vouch for the book; it has helped me in the ten-plus years since I first found out about David's extracurricular activities, and it continues to salve the small, smoldering inner wounds.

My therapist recommended *Women Who Run with the Wolves* to me in my first week of counseling with her. After that session, I went straight to the bookstore and bought it. I was desperate for anything that would help me understand what was going on with me, as well as with David and with us. As I read it, I underlined a lot of text meaningful to me. Even though it's been a while since I finished "studying" the book and marking segments, I still flip through it from time to time to help recapture some of the "magic." I'm not saying it worked wonders in my life, but it helped smooth out many of the rough spots, and that includes referring back to it nowadays if I hit a proverbial pothole.

Getting out of a marriage via divorce doesn't inoculate you from the stings and bruises produced by other bumps down the road when it comes to dating and new relationships—if you are into that sort of thing. There should be no pressure on you—and that includes self-inflicted pressure—to seek a new relationship commitment with a guy just for the sake of having one. No rush, regardless your age. Be true to yourself, and take care of yourself first. Look out for No. 1. Besides, a glass of wine and a hot soak in the tub—yes, by yourself—followed by a soft landing on the sofa in your jammies to watch a movie or read a book goes an awfully long way in the me-first healing process!

Meet Bluebeard

Early in her book, Estés discusses the fairy tale/fantasy character of Bluebeard, a wealthy and powerful nobleman. He's large and intimidating in stature, owns a large castle, and spends much of his life preying on women and luring them to his castle. When he gets them there, he holds them captive before killing them. Estés uses the character of Bluebeard to illustrate the "predator of the psyche," a force that lurks in the psyche of the women—as well as in men—and who "is instead filled with hatred and desires to kill the lights of the psyche."[1] One adaptation of the novel originally written in 1697 is the 1972 movie starring Richard Burton as the Bluebeard character and the likes of Raquel Welch, Joey Heatherton, and Sybil Danning in supporting roles. It's not Oscar material by any stretch, but if you ever care enough to dig up a copy of the movie, it gives you a pretty good idea of what we are dealing with.

Estés offers more explanation for the Bluebeard phenomenon when she writes:

> In psychological interpretation we call on all aspects of the fairy tale to represent the drama within a single woman's psyche. Bluebeard represents a deeply reclusive complex, which lurks at the edge of all women's lives, watching, waiting for an opportunity to oppose her. Although it may symbolize itself similarly or differently in men's psyches, it is the ancient and contemporary foe of both genders . . .

> It is not hard to imagine in such a malignant formation there is trapped one who once wished for surpassing light and fell from Grace because of it. . . . Both within and without, there is a force which will act in opposition to the instincts of the natural self, and that that malignant force *is what it is.* Though we might have mercy upon it, our first actions must be to recognize it, to protect ourselves from the devastations and ultimately to deprive it of its murderous energy.[2]

That second paragraph quoted above is one of the many segments that I had underlined in the book ten years before I started writing this one. Remember, this was material I was learning through reading and therapy while still married to David and in the early stages of what I was going through. I highly doubt David would have a clue who Bluebeard was.

Reading *Women Who Run with the Wolves* for the first time, and then reading back through it now, helps me understand not so much *why* but *that* my instincts were not intact during the last few years of our marriage. In hindsight, this was especially evident in the weeks and months of my discovery (through his admission, *finally*) of his affair. What I didn't know was why this was going on—not so much the *why* of his affair, but why, in retrospect, I hadn't been in possession of my instincts. Why wasn't I tapping into them and exercising them? What was I thinking?

I was in so much anguish at the time for David's not giving me the information I had been requesting as well as at least the basics of his affair—the who, what, when, where, and why. It was just eating away at me, and I was just blown away by the fact that I had missed it all. What this material in Estés's book did was help me better understand what my instincts were and why they weren't intact. It also helped explain how I could have been so naïve, how I could not have seen this. Yes, this was a great book for me, and I recommend it for you as well if you suspect you might be headed for divorce or already embroiled in one—after you finish reading this book, of course. ☺

Let me also add, in case you are wondering what I mean by instincts, here's another segment from Estés that helps bring clarification to what I am talking about here: "The Bluebeard story is about the captor, the dark man who inhabits all women's psyches, the innate predator. . . . To restrain the natural predator of the psyche it is necessary for women to remain in possession of all their instinctual powers. Some of these are insight, intuition, endurance, tenacious loving, keen sensing, far vision, acute hearing, singing over the dead, intuitive healing, and tending to their own creative fires."[3]

Let's suppose you are going through marriage difficulties for the first time, difficulties to the point that you are considering divorce after just finding out that your spouse is involved in an affair, whether it be with a woman or another man. Either way, the sanctity of your marriage commitment has been violated, and now you are in an emotional freefall.

If he won't talk about it, that's a big red flag beyond knowing that he's been cheating. It's possible for marriages to be saved after one spouse has had an affair (and either been caught in it or admitted to it). But it probably won't be saved if he is unwilling to talk about it. If he did, chances are good that, with the help of therapy or counseling, you could work it out and move forward from there. Now that I've been through this and received professional therapy specific to it, I believe the immediate reaction of the noncheating spouse, whether this is, in a clinical sense, considered "right" or "wrong," is to get all the details of the affair, as extremely painful as they might be to hear. It's important to know that they will hurt so that you can at least be prepared and have a fighting chance to handle them with a clear mind. This involves really listening to what's being said instead of being shocked out of your mind and unable to react rationally. I'm a full-disclosure kind of person, so I had to know the names, dates, and places (while plotting them on my own handy Thomas Kinkade calendar).

You can never be too prepared. My next piece of advice, if you have just found out about your spouse's affair, is to go see a therapist as soon as possible, first alone and then with your spouse. My aunt also suggested getting my own credit card and researching divorce lawyers as well. Let me repeat: You can never be too prepared. In such circumstances, it's virtually impossible for your life to continue on as it had been. This is a good thing. Meanwhile, do the best you can in terms of eating healthy foods and getting some form of exercise (cutting back on the alcohol [which includes wine] during this time!). I learned a lesson the hard way, embarrassing myself in the process (even though none of the witnesses had a clue who I was. Ha ha). As I demonstrated in living color, too much wine can lead to a public fight somewhere as inconspicuous as the Minneapolis airport, where, while waiting for a flight, I enjoyed several glasses of wine and ended up screaming, while sprinting to our gate, at my philandering husband loudly enough for the entire airport to hear about what he did. Ugh. It gives me pain just writing about it, and that was more than ten years ago. Let this be a lesson to you: even though your spouse might have chosen someone other than you to be his intimate partner, don't use this as an opportunity to damage yourself!

You can be naïve, maybe, by avoiding these hard discussions between wife and husband. Like in my case, not sitting down and talking through—I was willing—why we were unable to have our own child. Even if I had asked him to sit down and really talk about this, to confront him about this and not let it go until he spoke, that would have been really hard for him. Well, too bad. Tough. I missed that chance, and, no, I don't want the chance to relive that opportunity now that I know better. It is better I never see or talk to him again, at least on any topic related to our former relationship.

My instincts were not intact then. I think I understand and follow my instincts much better now. Otherwise, you can find yourself going down a path like I did, avoiding some things. Instincts are there to help you survive, to surround you with the right people—the ones who will support you. Instincts help you to ask the right questions and to find the answers quickly. I used to not listen to any of my instincts; now I do. They serve me so much better.

Another issue in all this, and it certainly pertains to me and my marriage—and it still does in my life as a single—is trust. I was too trusting, and now it takes years for me to get to the point where I trust someone after meeting them. And that's OK because I'm doing it in my own time and in my own way, and I'm trusting my own instincts. I'm working very hard to be less naïve, and *work* is the key word. You have to work at it. You have to work at trust, you have to work on yourself, and that is really difficult. That is work that I had never done before, and it remains a work in progress.

Wild Kingdom

This is a good place to take another brief detour again and refer back to the book *Women Who Run with the Wolves* and what I learned from it and how it still guides me today. Later in the book—well past the part where Estés introduces Bluebeard—she discusses "wild mothers" and having access to them. In my interpretation, that translates to surrounding yourself with a multitude of counsel. Says Estés, "These are women, who, as soon as you see them, something in you leaps, and something in you thinks, 'Mama.' You take one look and think, 'I am her progeny, I am her child, she is my mother, my grandmother.' They are like fairy godmother, like mentor, like the mother you never had, or did not have long enough . . ."[4]

Estés elaborates:

> All these human beings could be called little wild mothers. Usually everyone has at least one. If you are lucky, throughout a lifetime we will have several. You are usually grown or in your late adolescence by the time you meet them. They are vastly different from the too-good mother. The little wild mothers guide you, burst with pride over your accomplishments. They are critical of blockages and mistaken notions in and around your creative, sensual, spiritual, and intellectual life.

> Their purpose is to help you, to care about your art, and to reattach you to the wildish instincts, and to elicit your original best. They guide the restoration of the intuitive life. . . . [5]

Journaling is another part of this, the road to recovery, with the object of that recovery being the recovery of self. *Yourself.* As part of that, there's the 'what-if' and looking ahead. What do you have to look forward to, and it begins with finding something—anything—to pull yourself out of the abyss that you are in, like the one I was in. I'm talking about just writing in general—sitting down, taking pen in hand, and making that reconnection with yourself.

I still journal occasionally, but nothing like I did in 2007, 2008, and 2009, when all those waves and rough waters were crashing against the rocks in my head (pun intended). Those were hard times, but they were also great times in the sense that I became so connected to myself and living in the present. I am proof that even adversities in your life can turn into building blocks for your future contented, successful self. That doesn't seem possible at the time you are walking through that sort of slop, but I know it now as an experience that I wouldn't tempt the fates with going back in time to change any of it. It has made me a better person. It can do the same for you as well, but you have to take charge of that to make it happen—and to keep looking ahead with hope and positive expectations.

At the time I was going through this, I was also traveling—a lot. I've still got some of my high school friends. Plus I've got a college friend, and another group of friends that I'm close with. I'm very clear in thinking when I meet somebody that if they are someone I want to be friends with. Call it gut instinct or just being more assertive in my own mind, I can tell fairly quickly what works for me and what doesn't, and that pertains to people as much as it does to any other facet of my life.

Some form of that instinctual nature existed within me when I first met David, back in my early twenties. But I didn't have the knowledge or tools to exercise it, let alone to know that it even existed as described by Estés. Even then, I've always thought, to some extent, that David lacked class and integrity. It became very apparent later on in our marriage. I say it again to drive home the point: my instincts were not as sharp as they should have been. I was a far-too-trusting person. His father had cheated on his mother, and when he referenced that in promising to me he'd never do that to me—nor would he want to see anyone hurt as his mother had been—I truly felt completely safe.

If I could go back and talk to my younger self, and I guess I'm speaking this to you as well, I would say: "Take stock in what you have." I wanted it to be more profound, even though I never verbalized that to anyone, least of all David. I was a fool to let things go on as they did for as long as they did. Listen to yourself; do the hard work.

The old adage "Actions speak louder than words" should have been my mantra. It can be yours, though! Life was just moving so quickly for me. From day one, it moved far too quickly for me to actually enjoy it. There were new job opportunities, dinners out with colleagues, moves, new jobs, etc. All that was interesting (at first), although I remember feeling how strange it was that I wished for something to happen between us . . . for us to feel connected, engaged, two as one, etc. Yet, even with that sense of detachment, I could not have dreamed up this affair ever happening.

It has definitely affected me. It made me a lot more careful with friendships and relationships, and I've learned to be happy with myself, too. It worries me, too: I can choose to be alone or choose a life that is meant to be shared. I'm still trying to figure this out.

9

MoveOn.girl

MY BEST ADVICE TO ANYONE WHO HAS GONE THROUGH A DIVORCE and is looking to "get on with her life"— which can mean any one of a million things for the millions of American females who get unhitched every year—is to buy a few books, some really good, carefully chosen reads. Also, stock your pantry with plenty of wine; surround yourself with carefully vetted friends, old and new; get plenty of exercise; and travel—out of country if you can. You don't have to be anywhere close to wealthy to do any or all of those things, but they can all go a long way to properly recalibrate your life's direction.

It's also OK to love once again with a new significant other or two (preferably not at the same time), but know that even the second or third time around can turn out to be déjà vu all over again. Be forewarned: being not just burned but scorched in a relationship does not protect you from similar diseased relationships later in life. Just so you know, I came close to getting married a second time within a couple years, but I'll get back to that in a jiff.

I'm damn proud of myself that I left David. I could have stayed. It would have been really hard to stick with it, and it was super hard to leave, but it was my best move. Over time, I did a lot of the hard work sorting out the chaos and turbulence in my head and heart, and I continue to do the hard work of figuring out who I am and what I need because I don't think I had ever considered those things before.

Socially, I now have a great group of friends who love to read, travel, and drink wine, all of which are well within my comfort zone. The friends that I have and love back in the New Jersey area are my high school friends. My friends here in Tennessee have a lot of shared interests—and they listen to me.

I've always had friends, but when I moved to the West Coast, I started off not knowing anybody there, and, quite honestly, I never established many friends there, at least not good, solid ones. The group of friends I now have here in Memphis are mature and professional. I still keep in touch with all my other friends in other places. And I love being Aunt Rachel to my sister's three kids. I now realize the benefits of going through something difficult but making good choices and coming out ahead and happy on the other side.

I have a guy friend I've been dating for more than eight years, and we're both quite content with that relationship—each having our own home, but getting together often and doing a lot of things together. As I write this, that's my safe zone. To this day, though, I still have issues with trust, and that takes me back to what I said earlier in this chapter about how I almost got married two years after my divorce.

Déjà Vu

It's been an interesting journey. It might have been before my divorce was final that I started dating a dentist, about the same age as me. Somebody had set us up. He eventually professed his love for me, and we started talking about marriage. Then came a trip he took up to Martha's Vineyard in Massachusetts for a dental conference. Everything seemed fine for a while after he got back, but then I started getting phone calls a couple months later from a girl who told me she'd been talking to him and they had started a relationship. She told me he had told her about me, so she went looking for me, found me and my phone number, and called me.

"Did you know that he is also calling me?" she said.

Next time I saw him, I said, "You know everything that I have just been through—how could you have done that?" We had been going out for about a year, so we were pretty close. He was around for my fortieth birthday, which was big—and significant in our relationship—because all of my family flew in, so that was a huge breach of trust. I told him to get out of my life and never call me again, and that was it.

How can *you* prevent this? Maybe you can't control it early on, when you don't know about it yet, but *you* have control once you find out. Again, I had no idea this was happening with the dentist, because his hot babe lived in Virginia, about a thousand miles away from me. But she picked up the phone and called me. The choice at that point is yours: when you do find out, you should already know what you are going to do about it. Call it just another form of disaster preparedness.

Within about a year after that, a neighbor set me up with potential Love Connection No. 2. We went out a whole bunch of times. I'd hear from him and we'd go out to eat. There would be kissing, and then I wouldn't hear from him for weeks. I don't know; I guess I was too proud and didn't want to call him. It was weird. In the end, I had had enough of this back and forth, and the next time he called I said, "I'm done here."

It was literally like a year ago—as I write this, that Mr. Hot and Cold emailed me out of the blue. He said he really needed to talk to me because he needed to apologize for some things. It had been a few years since I had last seen him. I didn't know; maybe he was going through some counseling or something like that and needed to clear some slates. I was also thinking he might have been with someone else at the same time that he and I were getting together, off and on, and that would account for the amount of time that went by when I wouldn't hear from him. Some of these guys are so slick, at least the ones that I choose, that they get you coming and going. I suppose this was his way of re-entering my life to apologize to me, but *noooooo* apology accepted, even before he could explain. I said, "I don't know what you are going to tell me, but I've moved on." It's been interesting.

Those two experiences made me even more distrustful, but I have also known that life was meant to be shared. Absolutely. I just couldn't find the right guy. Now, I just like being alone. That's weird for me, but I've done a 180 here. Now in my early fifties, I'm listening to my heart as well as to my brain, and I'm taking it slow. Building in that time for meaningful discussion has been very good for me. I have a different focus now, and it's more about making life the best that it can be. Life is having good friends you can sit around with, having a glass of wine and generating new ideas. Only now do I feel like I'm really opening up to them. It takes a while to carve out this sort of thing. There should never be a rush.

I love my life and pretty much always have. I listen to my instincts now so much better than I ever have. I also like to travel, and now I get to do it without it being one of those business trips with David. The whole idea of traveling is now a different priority for me. Before, it was traveling for business, always paid for by David's company. Now I'm free and able to plan to do the things I want to do. If you're not doing this for yourself, you are missing out. Live a little; spend a little. Adventure travel is fun!

El Camino

One of the best post-drama trips I've had was one when I went to Spain with friends. That was in the summer of 2016, and we hiked through the last hundred miles of El Camino. If you do the whole hike, it's actually thirty days long, but I did the last week of it. That's more than ten miles a day, which can be really hard when you're drinking beer while walking in the morning hours. It tested every muscle in my body.

Along the way, we stayed in these beautiful little inns, homes, and a restored monastery. One night we stayed in someone's home and had dinner with them and their family. Along the way we hiked through fields and the little villages, and at times followed a dirt-lined path. When you're hiking El Camino, you might find yourself walking along with somebody from Australia. Then you might be walking with someone from France for a few hours, then you'd walk alone for a few hours. Everybody was on a journey. Or staving off a hangover. Before we started hiking part of El Camino, we frontloaded it a little too much in Madrid and Barcelona. We started off in the red. Drank too much sangria. Then again, having a beer first thing in the morning and eating octopus can really get you going.

Once we got to Santiago, one of the most beautiful cities in the world, we attended Mass with all the other pilgrims. Then, in our case at least, we got our certificate, drank a bunch of sangria, and got this really cool tattoo on our ankles. It's a scalloped shell, the symbol for El Camino. You had to follow this scalloped shell, depicting El Camino, as it took you along the route.

El Camino is a trail; some parts of it you are climbing, and some you are going down hills—and that's just the last part, what we covered over those seven days. The first part of El Camino begins in France, where you are hiking through the Pyrenees. There is a movie that best describes El Camino, which to this day stands as another life-changing event for me since the divorce. The movie

is called *The Way,* and it stars Martin Sheen and his son
Emilio Estevez. I won't say anything else about the
movie—you really need to see it—except that they hiked
El Camino.

It was a real test, gosh, and it was a wonderful way to
experience freedom. It was beautiful, and we were gross
all day long, but what a way to appreciate life and other
people and see what everyone else was doing. The first
thing you say when you greet someone new is *buen camino*—"a good walk." And the second thing you want to
say each time is, "Why are you here?" Sometimes it would
be a mother and daughter hiking before the daughter
went off to college; sometimes it would be a dad and a
son—everybody had a different reason for being there.

We were walking along and inside a little village we
saw a house that needed a new roof (as I did). Went a little
farther and we saw these little Styrofoam cartons of fresh
raspberries next to a little bottle of cream. Next to that
was a dilapidated basket and a little sign that said, in Spa-
nish, "We need a new roof." Next to it was another little
sign that said to take the raspberries and put in what we
could. We'd see a few of those along the way.

People in Spain are just amazing.

Donate . . . give back what you can because it can be
more about taking good care of yourself. Take good care
of others.

Cave Woman

Another life-changing event for me was going to Belize,
in Central America. I've now gone there three times—

each time with a bunch of friends from work. We do it as teachers, not as tourists so much, although we are soaking in sights, sounds, and people as we go. We land in Belize City and then drive west where we work in schools all morning, teaching kids and teachers. They have very little. We fill suitcases with things like crayons and dry erase markers. It's a fantastic thing to be able to do and to share what you know with them. Then, in the afternoon, we would go ziplining and explore the ATM (Actun Tunichil Muknal) cave, which is on *National Geographic*'s list of the top ten caves in the world to explore. There are a bunch of other really cool things to do in Belize.

Let me tell you about one time in particular about the ATM cave. It involved getting ourselves through a really small space—not for someone with even a smidgen of claustrophobia. One afternoon while exploring with a guide, we covered miles and miles inside, over this and down that. All along the way we listened to our guide's ghost stories and saw all this cutlery and the bones of people who had died in there.

It had rained the week before and, as we were leaving and on the way back out, we came to a place where our only way out was underwater. While we had been inside exploring, the water level had risen significantly, leaving just a small opening between the top of the water and the roof where we needed to pass under in order to exit the cave. Our only option was to submerge ourselves completely underwater, our heads and helmets (adorned with lights helping to lead the way) included, and we had

144

to push ourselves out of there. I can't really say our lives were in danger, though, as once we were submerged and pushing out, it was just a brief time with daylight not far away, but, yeah, we could feel the walls closing in on us. There were probably ten of us, and it was a shared experience that tells you that you can find great strength in a time of need, and that necessity is the mother of invention.

On My Own

A big part of my life continues to be running. I actually started running while in college. Then I stopped for a few years and instead did a lot of walking, and then got back into running while in New Jersey and continued doing it when we got to the West Coast. Thanks to running, all the things that are knocking around in my head seem to eventually drop into the right folders. Running has been a good outlet for me, and it could be for you, although walking might be better for you if the high-impact nature of running creates too much stress for your knees and/or feet. I highly recommend running, but be sure to have good running shoes, because I'm pretty sure that I've messed up my hips and knees from wearing shoes that weren't right for me. You want shoes with really good support. I prefer good running shoes, not cross trainers.

I've been asked if I regret not having had any children. No regrets. I get my fill of children every day in the classroom and with my sister Corinne's three kids. Little things do come up every once in a while where I'm wondering what it would be like if I had a child of my own, but I'm also several years past the stage in my life where I could have a child of my own; that's a realization that helps me cope.

There's nothing to miss now because nothing is going to happen, and you can move on from that. You really can. That's the good news: You can move on from everything; time heals all wounds, even though it might take a long, long time. I got out as soon as I could. Plus I continued with therapy for a few years after the divorce. I took good care of myself and others, and went right back to work. What does take a while is rebuilding your psyche, your trust. If you need help, go get it. Don't ever be reluctant to reach out for help from those who can give it to you, including professionals.

I refer back to my notes from the therapy sessions every once in a while, and the more I read over my journals, the more the information really sets in. Today's lesson: If you need therapy, it's nothing to be afraid of. In today's world, it's no longer a sign there is something wrong with you, that getting therapy makes you an outcast from society. It's called taking care of yourself, just like going to the doctor, a nutritionist, or a psychologist.

The same goes for your kids. A lot of people in my generation who have kids with problems don't want their kids talking to therapists. But therapy is a healthy thing to do, provided you do it with someone professionally qualified to be taking your life into their hands. Those kids who do speak to therapists are being given the tools that not many other people have. Being open-minded in that regard is so important. There shouldn't be any stigma attached to taking care of yourself, whether it be physical, psychological, emotional, or spiritual.

Bucket List

I do have a bucket list; one of the items on it is to continue with the bucket list—I just keep adding things to it. Like this summer (2020), I was planning to spend two weeks in Ireland, but as I write this, the coronavirus pandemic around the world is wreaking havoc with all kinds of schedules. More than anything, I want to be helpful to people. I want to help women and men who have been through this kind of relational trauma, and for this book to be helpful in some way.

Let me end this by saying that every marriage has its problems; you already knew that. At least I now know what the problems were with my marriage and what hindsight has taught me—both in regard to the immediacy of finding out, like I did that spring morning in California, and then in what followed over the months and years since. In my case that included the abbreviated attempt at reconciliation, the divorce, and my life as a single person that continues to this day. Whether you are in a good marriage or a bad one, I suggest you develop a guard/warrior attitude for yourself! Just like I described in chapter 8 where I discussed several salient points covered in the book *Women Who Run with the Wolves*. Define for yourself ahead of time what the repercussions will be if your needs aren't met (and your spouse should do the same, of course; it works both ways). I also learned that a person in a bad marriage relationship needs to be prepared to clean up things for herself or himself.

It's never too late to develop a guard/warrior attitude. That means being prepared, planning ahead, and having your hazmat suit ready. Overcoming challenges creates new life.

Today the betrayal proves to be the most difficult thing to get past, with the more difficult work being to focus on who I am and my needs. I still grieve over memories of our marriage, but leaving California and that sordid mess behind was the smartest thing I have ever done.

Resources

Chapter 3: Baby, Baby

1. Mayo Clinic, "In Vitro Fertilization," https://www.mayoclinic.org/tests-procedures/in-vitro-fertilization/about/pac-20384716, viewed August 6, 2019.

2. Mayo Clinic.

3. Mayo Clinic.

4. Mayo Clinic.

5. Merrill, Elizabeth, "IVF Failure Is Devastating and More Common Than You Think," www.huffpost.com, https://www.huffpost.com/entry/opinion-merrill-ivf-failure_n_5adf8637e4b061c0bfa27b19, viewed August 6, 2019.

6. Merrill.

7. Merrill.

Chapter 6: Reconciliation: Failure to Launch

1. Snyder, Douglas K. PhD; Donald H. Baucom, PhD; and Kristina Coop Gordon, PhD, *Getting Past the Affair: A Program to Help You Cope, Heal, and Move On—Together or Apart*. New York: The Guilford Press, 2007, p. 175.

2. Snyder, Baucom, and Gordon, pp. 176–177.

3. Snyder, Baucom, and Gordon, p. 210.

4. Snyder, Baucom, and Gordon, p. 220.

5. Snyder, Baucom, and Gordon, pp. 220–221.

Chapter 7: The Divorce

1. Snyder, Douglas K. PhD; Donald H. Baucom, PhD; and Kristina Coop Gordon, PhD, *Getting Past the Affair: A Program to Help You Cope, Heal, and Move On—Together or Apart*. New York: The Guilford Press, 2007, p. 308.

Chapter 8: The Wild Woman

1. Estés, Clarissa Pinkola, PhD, *Women Who Run with the Wolves: Myths and Stories of the Wild Woman Archetype*. New York: Ballantine Books, 1993, p. 45.

2. Estés, pp. 44–45.

3. Estés, pp. 43–44.

4. Estés, p. 119.

5. Estés, p. 119.

The Author

RACHEL SPRY IS THE PSEUDONYM for a school teacher who lives in the southern part of the United States and who recently passed the ten-year mark since her divorce. This is her first book.

Notes

Notes

Notes

Notes

Notes

Made in the USA
Middletown, DE
13 March 2021